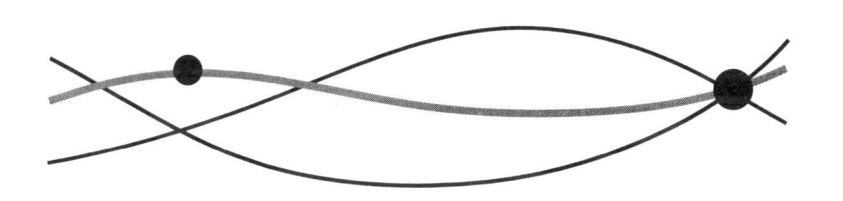

# DANIEL, HOSEA, AND JOEL

## MESSAGES OF RENEWAL, INTIMACY, AND PROPHETIC HOPE

# Light to My Path Series

## Old Testament

*Ezra, Nehemiah, and Esther*
*Job*
*Isaiah*
*Jeremiah and Lamentations*
*Ezekiel*
*Daniel, Hosea, and Joel*
*Amos, Obadiah, and Jonah*
*Micah, Nahum, Habakkuk, and Zephaniah*
*Haggai, Zechariah, and Malachi*

## New Testament

*John*
*Acts*
*Romans*
*1 Corinthians*
*2 Corinthians*
*Galatians and Ephesians*
*Philippians and Colossians*
*James and 1 & 2 Peter*
*The Epistles of John and Jude*

# Daniel, Hosea, and Joel

**Messages of Renewal, Intimacy, and Prophetic Hope**

F. Wayne Mac Leod

**Authentic**

Authentic Publishing
We welcome your questions and comments.

USA   PO Box 444, 285 Lynnwood Ave, Tyrone, GA, 30290
authentic@stl.org or www.authenticbooks.com
UK   9 Holdom Avenue, Bletchley, Milton Keynes, Bucks, MK1 1QR, UK
www.authenticmedia.co.uk
India   Logos Bhavan, Medchal Road, Jeedimetla Village,
Secunderabad 500 055, A.P.

Daniel, Hosea, and Joel
ISBN-10: 1-932805-75-3
ISBN-13: 978-1-932805-75-8

Copyright © 2005 by F. Wayne Mac Leod

09 08 07 06 / 6 5 4 3 2 1

Published in 2006 by Authentic
All rights reserved. No part of this book may be reproduced in any form without permission in writing from the publisher, except in the case of brief quotations embodied in critical articles or reviews.

Unless otherwise noted, all Scripture is taken from the HOLY BIBLE, NEW INTERNATIONAL VERSION ®. Copyright © 1973, 1978, 1984 by International Bible Society. Used by permission of Zondervan Publishing House. All rights reserved.

Scripture quotations marked "NKJV" are taken from the New King James Version. Copyright © 1982 by Thomas Nelson, Inc. Used by permission. All rights reserved.

Cover design: Paul Lewis
Interior design: Angela Lewis
Editorial team: Bette Smythe, Megan Kassebaum, Dana Carrington

Printed and bound in India by
OM Authentic Media, P.O.Box 2190, Secunderabad 500 003
E-mail: printing@ombooks.org

# Contents

Preface ... 1

## Daniel

1. Faithful in Small Things ... 5
   *Read Daniel 1:1–21*
2. The King's Dream ... 10
   *Read Daniel 2:1–49*
3. Nebuchadnezzar's Golden Idol ... 18
   *Read Daniel 3:1–30*
4. The Humbling of Nebuchadnezzar ... 23
   *Read Daniel 4:1–37*
5. Writing on the Wall ... 31
   *Read Daniel 5:1–31*
6. In the Lions' Den ... 36
   *Read Daniel 6:1–28*
7. The Four Beasts ... 41
   *Read Daniel 7:1–28*
8. The Ram and the Goat ... 51
   *Read Daniel 8:1–27*
9. Daniel's Prayer ... 57
   *Read Daniel 9:1–27*
10. Michael and the Persians ... 63
    *Read Daniel 10:1–21*
11. The Angel's Revelation: From Darius to Seleucus IV ... 69
    *Read Daniel 11:1–20*
12. The Angel's Revelation: Antiochus IV Epiphanes ... 75
    *Read Daniel 11:21–45*
13. The Final Victory ... 81
    *Read Daniel 12:1–13*

## Hosea

| | |
|---|---:|
| 14. Introducing the Prophet<br>*Read Hosea 1:1–11* | 89 |
| 15. The Discipline of a Loving Father<br>*Read Hosea 2:1–15* | 94 |
| 16. Reconciliation<br>*Read Hosea 2:16–3:5* | 99 |
| 17. Sowing Seeds of Evil<br>*Read Hosea 4:1–5* | 104 |
| 18. Accusations against the Priests<br>*Read Hosea 4:6–14* | 108 |
| 19. Bad Company<br>*Read Hosea 4:15–19* | 112 |
| 20. Guilty!<br>*Read Hosea 5:1–15* | 116 |
| 21. False Piety<br>*Read Hosea 6:1–11* | 120 |
| 22. Israel's Crime<br>*Read Hosea 6:11–7:16* | 125 |
| 23. Fruitless Faith<br>*Read Hosea 8:1–14* | 131 |
| 24. Israel's Punishment<br>*Read Hosea 9:1–17* | 136 |
| 25. It is Time to Seek the Lord<br>*Read Hosea 10:1–15* | 142 |
| 26. Grace in Rebellion<br>*Read Hosea 11:1–12* | 148 |
| 27. More Sin<br>*Read Hosea 12:1–14* | 152 |
| 28. Rebellious Ephraim<br>*Read Hosea 13:1–16* | 158 |
| 29. The Conclusion of the Matter<br>*Read Hosea 14:1–9* | 163 |

## Joel

| | |
|---|---|
| 30. Victory in Humility<br>*Read Joel 1:1–20* | 169 |
| 31. The Approaching Army<br>*Read Joel 2:1–11* | 174 |
| 32. Return to Me<br>*Read Joel 2:12–27* | 179 |
| 33. The Outpouring of the Spirit<br>*Read Joel 2:28–32* | 184 |
| 34. The Valley of Jehoshaphat<br>*Read Joel 3:1–16* | 189 |
| 35. A Bright Future for God's People<br>*Read Joel 3:17–21* | 194 |

# Preface

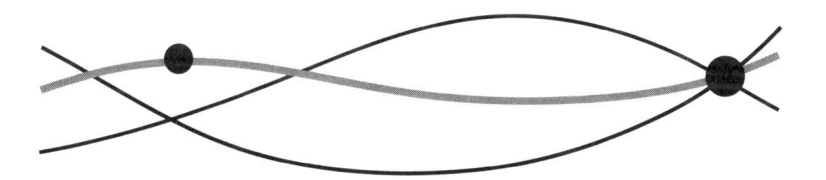

The prophet Daniel spoke to a people in exile who were paying the price for their sin. Even while in exile for their rebellion, God's people still knew his presence and blessing. The book of Daniel is the story of a man who stood out in the midst of a rebellious people and who was unashamed of his God. It shows us that while God will not abandon his people, he will discipline them for their own good.

Hosea is a prophecy to a nation that turned its back on God. It is a story of a God who patiently endured insults and rebellion. The book serves as a warning to all who read it that the Lord is a God of holiness and justice. Hosea reminds us that God will deal with sin. God's people, like the prodigal son, had wandered far from him, and they suffered the consequences of their rebellion. God did not forsake them, however. He waited, with arms open wide, to receive them. Through the prophet Hosea, God called his people back to himself. The prophecy is a story of the grace of God in dealing with those who have wandered from him.

In the prophecy of Joel, we see God's people moving from barrenness to spiritual revival and from devastation by locusts to a land flowing with new wine. We catch a glimpse of the merciful and compassionate heart of God as he poured out his Holy Spirit and blessings on a repentant people. The prophecy offers hope of renewal for all God's people.

This commentary is not meant to replace the Bible. It serves only as a guide to take you section by section through the prophecies of Daniel, Hosea, and Joel. Read the passages indicated at the beginning of each chapter. Work through the passage with the commentary, using it as a guide. Ask the Spirit of God to reveal the truth of the passage to you. You could possibly read one section each day in your personal quiet time with the Lord. Each chapter ends with a set of questions. Take a moment to reflect on these questions. They will help you think about the practical application of the passage. Conclude your time by praying about the things you have learned. I have also given some suggested prayer requests at the end of each chapter. Take a moment to pray over these requests.

My prayer is that this book will be instrumental in helping you walk devotionally through the prophesies of Daniel, Hosea, and Joel. This book not only seeks to help you understand the passage but also to see its practical application to your life. May God bless you over the next few weeks as you meditate on these important Scriptures.

F. Wayne Mac Leod

# Daniel

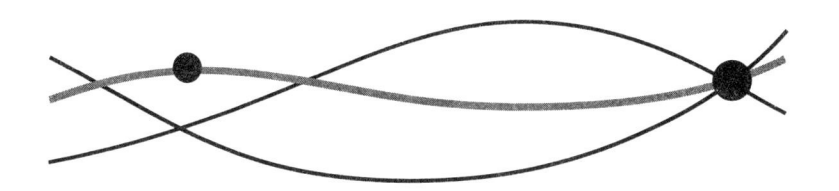

# 1
# Faithful in Small Things

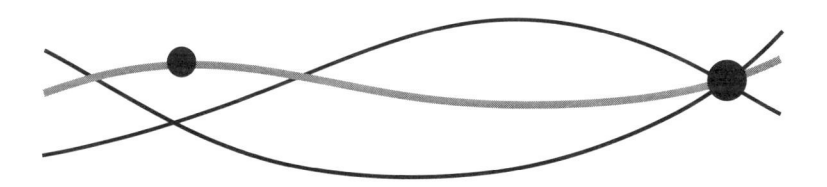

*Read Daniel 1:1–21*

The book of Daniel was written in a time of exile. The story of Daniel occurs during the reign of Nebuchadnezzar, king of Babylon. Commentators tell us that the events of this first chapter occurred while Daniel was just a youth. We are told that the training of youths for the service of the king took place usually before the child was twelve years of age. If this is the case, we must certainly admire the commitment of Daniel, even as a young man. The hand of God was on him from the beginning.

We begin the book of Daniel with some history of the period. It was in the third year of the reign of Jehoiakim of Judah that Nebuchadnezzar of Babylon came to Jerusalem and surrounded the city with his army (ca. 605 BC). At that time the Lord delivered Jehoiakim into the hands of Nebuchadnezzar. As an expression of victory, the king of Babylon took some of the articles from the temple in Jerusalem and placed them in the temple of his god in Babylon. These articles had been consecrated to the Lord God. This was a very difficult time of judgment for the people of God. They did not understand why the Lord had allowed this to happen. There would have been many questions on their minds.

Nebuchadnezzar also ordered the chief of the court officials to bring some young male Israelites into his court for training as court servants. These youths were to be of the noble class of Israelite society (verse 3). They were to be young men who were physically in perfect condition, handsome, and intelligent. We have already stated that very likely these captives would have been around twelve to fourteen years of age.

These youths were to be taught how to serve in the king's palace. Ashpenaz, the chief of the court officials, was to train them in the language and literature of Babylon (verse 4). Part of the training involved a special diet from the king's table. The training would last for a period of three years, and then these young men would enter into the service of the king of Babylon.

The book of Daniel tells us the story of four young Israelites chosen to be the king's court servants: Daniel, Hananiah, Mishael, and Azariah. They were given new Babylonian names when they entered their training. The name Daniel means "God is my judge." His name was changed to Belteshazzar, meaning "Bel's prince." Bel was a Babylonian god. By changing Daniel's name, the Babylonians intended for Daniel to worship the local gods. It is significant to note that Daniel chose to refer to himself by his Hebrew name rather than by his Babylonian name.

The names of Daniel's friends were also changed. Hananiah means "whom Jehovah has favored." His name was changed to Shadrach, after the Babylonian god Rak. Mishael, whose name means "who is comparable to God," was given the new name Meshach, after Shak, the goddess of love. Azariah's name means "Jehovah helps." He was given the name Abednego, meaning "servant of the shining fire." This could be a reference to the sun, an object of Babylonian worship.

In verse 8 we discover another way in which Daniel determined to remain committed to his God. Daniel resolved in his heart not to defile himself with the food and wine that came from the king's table. As a Jew, he understood that this food was unclean, according to the dietary laws of the Mosaic code. He determined in his heart that he would be obedient to the Lord in this matter and remain clean before God. Risking his life, he asked permission not to defile himself by eating unclean food.

This would not have been an easy decision for Daniel to make. He did not know what the response of the official would be to this request. What is clear from verse 9, however, is that the Lord gave him favor with the official. As Daniel chose to obey the Lord in this matter, the Lord blessed and provided a way of obedience for him. What is quite amazing here is to see how the official opened his heart to Daniel. He admitted to this young lad that he was afraid of the king's response if he found Daniel looking worse than the other boys. I find it quite interesting that this official would open his heart to Daniel about this matter. He was sympathetic toward Daniel's situation but did not want to risk shirking his responsibility as an official. This shows us something of how strict life in the court really was. The chief official feared for his life if he chose to disobey the direct command of the king and so did not give Daniel permission.

Seeing the hesitation of the official, Daniel made a decision by faith (verse 11). He believed that if he was obedient, the Lord would bless him. He asked the guard appointed by the chief official to test him and his friends for ten days on vegetables and water alone. (It is uncertain if the chief official, Ashpenaz, was aware of this.) At the end of ten days, the guard was to compare Daniel and his friends with the others who had been eating the king's food. We can only admire this kind of faith on the part of these Hebrew captives.

Verse 15 tells us that at the end of ten days, Daniel and his friends looked healthier and better nourished than the men who ate the king's food. Seeing this, the guard in charge of Daniel and his friends took away the king's food and fed them vegetables and water only. We cannot underestimate the impact that this had on the guard. Obviously, he would have seen the hand of God on the lives of these young men. Though they did not preach to him, their lifestyle and their obedience to God were a powerful testimony.

Notice that God blessed the obedience of Daniel and his friends in a wonderful way. Verse 17 tells us that the Lord gave them knowledge and understanding of all kinds of literature and learning in Babylon. This was a gift from God. To Daniel he gave another gift—that of understanding and interpreting dreams and visions. At this point in his life, Daniel would not have understood how important that gift would be.

At the end of three years of training, the king talked with each of the men who had been placed under the training of Ashpenaz, his chief court official. Nebuchadnezzar was very impressed with Daniel and his three friends. He found them ten times wiser than even the magicians and enchanters of his kingdom (verse 20). Daniel captured the attention of the king and was placed in the king's service. Daniel would serve in Babylon until the first year of Cyrus, king of Persia, when the children of Israel would return to their own land.

What we need to notice here is the obedience of Daniel in small things. He chose to be faithful in the matter of only eating what the Lord required of him. This act of self-discipline was blessed of God. What would have happened if Daniel had not been faithful to the Lord in this matter? Obedience in this simple matter was the first test Daniel needed to pass. Having passed this test, the Lord blessed him in abundance and released him into a fuller blessing. Daniel is an example of how a believer can remain faithful to the Lord in very difficult circumstances. May we be found faithful as well in the circumstances of our lives.

*For Consideration:*

- What was the connection between obedience and the blessing of God in the life of Daniel?

- Are there areas in your life where you still need to prove faithful?

- Have you ever found yourself making compromises and not being absolutely faithful?

- What do we learn about the faith of Daniel in this passage? How does your faith compare?

- What does this passage have to teach us about how God can use young people to witness for him?

*For Prayer:*

- Ask the Lord to reveal to you any area where you have failed to be as faithful as Daniel.

- Ask the Lord to give you more faith in him and his purposes.

- Thank the Lord that as we obey he will be faithful to us, as he was to Daniel.

# 2
# The King's Dream

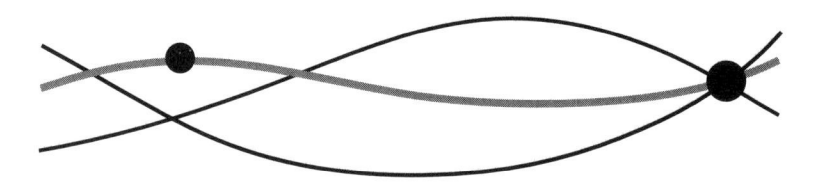

*Read Daniel 2:1–49*

Verse 1 tells us that in the second year of his reign, Nebuchadnezzar had a dream that troubled him very much. He called his magicians, sorcerers, enchanters, and astrologers to stand before him. It is striking that he would call such a number of them together. In normal conditions the king might have consulted one or two of the wise men, but there was something quite different about this dream.

When the wise men and magicians were gathered before him, the king told them that he had a dream that had troubled him and asked them to interpret it for him. When the astrologers asked the king to tell them his dream, the king refused to do so. He told them that they were not only to interpret his dream but also to tell him what he had dreamed. He warned them that if they could not tell him the dream, he would have them cut into pieces and their houses turned into piles of rubble (verse 5). If, on the other hand, they told him the dream and its interpretation, they would receive from him great gifts, rewards, and honor.

It is quite clear from this that the king was very troubled by this dream. He believed that this dream contained a message for him, and he did not want to miss that message. He needed to be sure that what the magicians and sorcerers said was true. The way he could tell if the interpretation was correct was by demanding that they also tell him what he had dreamed. This way he could confirm what was being said.

It is interesting to note here that the original text changes from Hebrew to Aramaic in this section of Daniel. While almost all of the Old Testament was written in Hebrew, this portion, from Daniel 2:4 to the end of chapter 7 was originally written in Aramaic. This unique section of Scripture contains prophecies concerning the Gentile nations.

The astrologers and those present were shocked at the king's request. Again they asked him to tell them the dream. Interpreting a dream was one thing, but telling the king what he dreamed was another. Again the king refused and accused them of trying to gain time because they did not have an answer (verse 8). He reminded them that their penalty would be very severe if they did not also tell him what he dreamed.

In verse 10 the astrologers told the king that there was no man on earth that could do such a thing. They also reminded him that there was never a king who asked so much from his magicians and astrologers. They were obviously hoping that the king would change his mind. "What the king asks is too difficult," they said. "No one can reveal it to the king except the gods, and they do not live among men" (verse 11). The king was asking them to fulfill their office and provide him with supernatural information, but this was something that was beyond their ability. They also knew that there was no way of deceiving the king this time with a contrived interpretation. If they did not perfectly guess the dream, they would be killed. These stakes were too high for them.

The king became so angry with these wise men that he ordered the execution of every wise man in Babylon (verse 12). This shows us how troubled by this dream the king re-

The King's Dream ● 11

ally was. It also shows us something of the power he had as king of Babylon. His decree was not questioned. Guards were immediately sent out to round up the wise men for execution (verse 13).

Daniel and his friends were considered to be among the wise men of the land. When Arioch, the commander of the king's guard, came to get Daniel and his friends, to put them to death, Daniel spoke to him about what was happening. Notice in verse 14 that he spoke "with wisdom and tact." He asked the Arioch why the king had issued such a harsh decree, and Arioch explained the situation to him. When Daniel heard what had happened, he went to the king and asked him for time so that he could interpret the king's dream.

There are a couple of things that we need to mention here. First, we see the influence of Daniel at this point. He had gained the favor and respect of the king in chapter 1. This favor was bearing fruit for Daniel. The fact that the king would grant him this request is an indication of just how much Daniel had gained his respect. It should be remembered that in chapter 1 the king found Daniel and his friends to be ten times wiser than all the magicians and wise men of the land.

The second thing we need to notice is that Daniel was not present when the wise men were summoned by the king. He was unaware of the situation when the guard came to get him for execution. This is significant. The king saw how his magicians could not answer his request. He would see Daniel's God do what none of his magicians and sorcerers could do. There would be no doubt that the God of Daniel was more powerful than the gods of Babylon. Had Daniel been included with the Babylonian magicians and wise men, the glory may have gone to Babylonian magic and not to the God of Israel. God made a dramatic distinction between the gods of Babylon and himself and between Babylon's wise men and Daniel.

Third, we need to see the boldness and faith of Daniel in this passage. He was not afraid to trust God in this situation. When everyone else failed, Daniel was willing to trust God for the solution. This took a very special faith.

The king granted Daniel his request for more time. When Daniel returned from speaking to the king, he explained the matter to his friends and urged them to pray and seek the favor of God (verse 18). Daniel knew that the answer would not come from human wisdom. The only way they would remain alive was if the Lord God showed his mercy and favor and revealed the king's dream and its interpretation. God honored this dependent faith and revealed to Daniel the dream that very night.

When God revealed the dream to him, Daniel was moved to praise and glorify the Lord. He knew that his prayer had been answered and that God had come to him that night. I'm sure Daniel didn't get much sleep that night. Instead, he spent the time praising the Lord. His words are recorded for us in verses 20–23.

Daniel praised the Lord for his wisdom and power (verse 20). He recognized God as the one who changes times and seasons. In other words, God controls world events and determines the duration of each phase of history. Daniel praised the Lord as the God who sets kings in place and deposes them as he sees fit (verse 21). Even King Nebuchadnezzar would be taken from his throne in God's sovereign time. Daniel revealed his faith that God controls all nations and was in control of Judah's exile in Babylon. Daniel thanked God for giving wisdom to the wise and knowledge to the discerning. All wisdom and knowledge come from God who reveals the deep and hidden things (verse 22). He knows what is hidden in the dark. Daniel concluded his time of praise with thanksgiving to the Lord God for having given him wisdom and power. He thanked the Lord for having made known to him what the king had dreamed.

It wasn't until after this time of worship and praise to God that Daniel went to Arioch and asked to see the king. Arioch told the king that he had found someone who could interpret his dream. It is significant that he particularly mentioned here that Daniel was one of the exiles from Judah. This immediately associated him with the God of Israel (verse 25). God was interested in lifting up his name in the eyes of Nebuchadnezzar.

The king asked Daniel if he could tell him what he saw in the dream and interpret it. Daniel was careful not to take any credit for himself. He told the king that there was no man or diviner who could explain what the king saw that night in his sleep. The Babylonian wise men tried to gain information about the future through astrology—the study of the movement of stars and planets. But Daniel told the king that the true revealer of mysteries is the "God in heaven" (verse 27). That God is the God of Israel. Daniel told Nebuchadnezzar that this God had revealed to him the king's dream and its interpretation. Daniel made sure that all the glory went to the Lord God of Israel. Daniel took no glory for himself.

In verse 29 Daniel spoke about the dream to the king. He told him that the dream related to things that were yet to happen. Before telling the king the details of the dream, Daniel reminded him that it was not because he had greater wisdom than other men that he understood this matter. The only reason Daniel knew the king's dream was because the Lord his God had revealed it to him.

How easy it is for us to take credit for ourselves or believe that God somehow needs our great wisdom and knowledge. Daniel was humble enough to be a simple vessel through whom God spoke. He claimed no special wisdom or power of his own. All glory went to his God. How we need to be more like Daniel in our personal lives. All too often, we want credit for ourselves. God is looking for those who are empty and willing vessels, totally dependent on him. God found that humility in Daniel.

In verses 31–35 Daniel described to the king what he had dreamed. He told Nebuchadnezzar that he had seen a statue that was enormous and dazzling. The head was made of pure gold; its chest and arms were made of silver; and its belly and thighs were crafted of bronze. The legs of the statue were iron, and the feet were partly iron and partly clay. As the king watched, a great rock struck the statue's feet, and the rest of the statue tumbled down and broke in pieces. The golden head, the silver chest, and the bronze belly were all smashed. The rock crushed the statue into dust that was blown away, leaving no trace. As for the rock, it became a huge mountain that seemed to fill the whole earth.

Having told the dream to King Nebuchadnezzar, Daniel proceeded to interpret it (verse 36). Nebuchadnezzar (represented by the gold head) was the king of kings. He was the most powerful king on the earth. Daniel reminded him, however, that his power and might had been given to him by the Lord God (verse 37). This God had placed humans, beasts, and the birds of the air into the king's hands. It is important to note here that the Lord sometimes gives his authority to unbelieving kings and rulers. He does this with a particular purpose in mind.

Daniel reminded Nebuchadnezzar that after him another kingdom would arise that was not as powerful as his—this was the kingdom of silver. Next, a third kingdom would arise, represented by bronze. The fourth kingdom (iron) would crush and break the other nations. While this nation would be powerful, it would not have the glory of Nebuchadnezzar's golden kingdom. The kingdom of iron would be divided. This was represented in the feet that were a mixture of iron and clay, which do not mix.

The day was coming, Daniel told Nebuchadnezzar, when the Lord God of heaven would set up still another kingdom that would never be destroyed. This kingdom would not be given to another nation. No nation would ever be able to conquer this final kingdom, and it would last forever (verse 44). This kingdom was represented by the rock that became as huge as a mountain. Even as this rock was not formed with human hands, so this kingdom would not be made by human hands. This was a kingdom of which God himself would be the creator and ruler.

Many commentators note that after Babylon came the kingdom of the Medes and the Persians. Some associate the

Medo-Persian Empire with the silver portion of the statue. Following the Medes and the Persians, Greece became a mighty power. It is associated with the bronze belly. Rome eventually conquered the Greek Empire and became the dominant world power. It is interesting to note that the Romans were a military people and, like iron, crushed other nations. Rome experienced much disunity and eventually fell. The kingdom made without human hands may very well be the kingdom that the Lord Jesus, himself would set up. We are part of that spiritual kingdom. It is not an earthly kingdom, but it is a kingdom where Jesus reigns. This kingdom will last forever, and no force will ever be able to conquer it. This kingdom of God is growing every day. Satan and all his hosts have done much to defeat it, but they have never been able to overcome. (Some Christians believe that this final kingdom has a physical aspect that will begin when the Lord Jesus returns and sets up an earthly kingdom that will last a thousand years.)

Having shared this interpretation with the king, Daniel reassured him that the dream was from the Lord, and it was intended to show him the things that were to come. Daniel assured the king that the interpretation of the dream was fully trustworthy (verse 45).

When the king heard the interpretation, he fell prostrate before Daniel and honored him. The king knew that what he had heard was from the Lord. He may also have been very much relieved to hear that the dream was in his favor and that he had nothing to worry about during his reign. He ordered that offerings and incense be presented to Daniel. King Nebuchadnezzar knew that Daniel's God was the God of gods and the Lord of kings. The king realized that the God of Israel is the one who reveals mysteries. That day the king placed Daniel in a very high position in the land and gave him many gifts. Daniel became the ruler over the province of Babylon and head of all the wise men in the land. Daniel requested that his three friends also be given appointments by the king as administrators over Babylon (verse 49). This was granted.

As we look at this story before us, we are struck by the way the Lord moved to place his servant Daniel in power, even in the foreign country of his exile. By his bold confidence and faith in God, Daniel testified that the Lord his God is Lord of all lords and King of all kings and controls world history. Daniel's faith did not waver as he stood before the king. He expected God to do great things. He gave God the glory for all that happened, and God honored his faith, obedience, and humility.

*For Consideration:*

- What do we learn here about Daniel's faith in God? How did Daniel demonstrate boldness in faith? What is the challenge here for us?

- Is there a connection between Daniel's faithfulness to God and God's honoring him before the king?

- What does this chapter teach us about being empty vessels that God can use?

- In Daniel we see a balance of boldness and humility. Why is it important to find this balance in ministry?

*For Prayer:*

- Thank God that he is above every other god.

- Thank him that he is the giver of all wisdom and power.

- Ask the Lord to give you some of the boldness and humility of Daniel.

- Ask God to help you to trust him more. Ask him to forgive you for the times you did not give him all the glory for what he did in you and through you.

- Take a moment to thank the Lord Jesus for his kingdom that will never end. Thank him that you can have the assurance that you are part of that kingdom.

# 3

# Nebuchadnezzar's Golden Idol

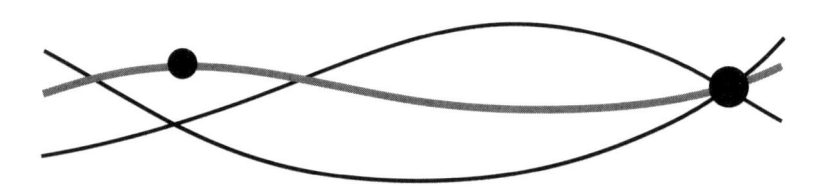

*Read Daniel 3:1–30*

In the last meditation, we saw how King Nebuchadnezzar had a dream about a large idol with a head of gold. Daniel revealed that Nebuchadnezzar was that head of gold. It may not be without coincidence that we see Nebuchadnezzar building a large statue of gold in chapter 3. Was he thinking of his dream when he built this statue? Verse 1 tells us that the statue was ninety feet high (twenty-seven meters) and nine feet wide (almost three meters). This was quite an undertaking.

When the statue was erected, Nebuchadnezzar called his leaders and officials together for the dedication of his image. All his officials came to the dedication and stood before the great statue. When everyone was present, a herald of the king made an announcement. He commanded that all the representatives of the various conquered nations present that day were to bow down and worship the image when the sound of the music began. Nebuchadnezzar ordered that anyone who did not follow this decree be thrown into a blazing furnace. To disobey his command was to die.

According to verse 7, when the music began the people who had gathered from the various nations fell down and worshiped the image of gold that Nebuchadnezzar had set up. This demonstrated their devotion to him as their ruler and their allegiance to the Babylonian Empire. Refusal to bow down would be seen as a crime of treason.

We understand from verse 8 that certain Jews refused to bow down to this image. This did not go unnoticed by the astrologers. They reported the matter to the king. They seemed quite eager to denounce these Jews. Could it be that they were jealous because Daniel and his friends had been given authority over them?

It is unclear where Daniel was at this time. He is not mentioned in this chapter. This leads some to believe that he was not present at this ceremony, perhaps because of illness or governmental business elsewhere.

Nebuchadnezzar was furious when he heard that Daniel's friends refused to obey his command. Shadrach, Meshach, and Abednego were brought before the king. Nebuchadnezzar offered them a second chance to bow down to the image. This may have been because of their high position in his government. They were certainly a very valuable asset to the king as wise men whom he could trust to tell him the truth. Nebuchadnezzar told them that when the music played again, he expected them to bow down and worship the image, or they would be thrown into the furnace. "What god will be able to rescue you from my hand?" he asked in verse 15.

There are a couple of things that we need to see in this statement of King Nebuchadnezzar. First, there is a hint here that Nebuchadnezzar recognized the God of the Israelites. He had already seen God's great wisdom in the interpretation of his dream. He had seen that the God of Israel had wisdom greater than all the Babylonian gods. He doubted, however, that the God of the Israelites was big enough to deliver these young men from his furnace.

This leads to a second observation about the king's statement. There is tremendous pride in what Nebuchadnezzar said here. He believed that he was more powerful than the gods. "What god can deliver you from my hand?" he asked. He did not understand the power of the God of Israel. He believed that God himself could not overturn his decision.

Shadrach, Meshach, and Abednego listened to the king and replied, "We do not need to defend ourselves before you in this matter" (verse 16). They were not interested, at this point, in a debate about whether God would deliver them or not. They simply committed themselves into his hands and did not try to defend themselves. They did not seek to persuade the king to change his mind by recalling all the good they had done for him in the past. Like the Lord Jesus, they stood silent before their accuser. God would be their defender. They knew that God was able to save them from the furnace, but, if he didn't and chose to allow them to suffer death, they would not bow the knee to the king's statue and dishonor the name of the God they loved and served. This matter was not open for discussion. They were more than willing to die. They would not compromise their faith. They cast themselves completely on God and chose to be obedient to death.

King Nebuchadnezzar was furious with Shadrach, Meshach, and Abednego. Verse 19 tells us that his attitude toward them changed. Up until this point, he was willing to give them a second chance. He was being merciful to them. Now, however, there would be no more chances. Instead, he ordered that the furnace be heated seven times hotter than usual. He called on some of his strongest soldiers to tie up Shadrach, Meshach, and Abednego and throw them into the furnace. They were bound in their robes and turbans and thrown into the furnace. The scorching heat killed the soldiers who threw the three men into the furnace.

As the king watched to see what would happen, he noticed something very strange (verse 24). He noticed, to his amazement, that there appeared to be a fourth person in the furnace. The appearance of the fourth person was very unusual. This person looked like "a son of the gods" (verse 25). What was particularly strange was that all four men were walking around in the furnace, unharmed and unbound. There in the midst of the furnace, Daniel's three friends met the Lord. The sense of his presence would have been very real and powerful. That same Lord is able to meet you too in your difficulty. Shadrach, Meshach, and Abednego were willing to obey to the end. God rewarded that obedience by his wonderful presence with them.

In verse 26 Nebuchadnezzar approached the furnace and called out to Daniel's three friends. Notice that he called them the "servants of the Most High God." He commanded that they come out of the furnace. This time they obeyed the king's order and came out of the furnace. The governors and royal officials crowded around to see what had become of them. Not a hair on their heads was singed. Their clothes were not burned, nor was there even a scent of fire on them. God had completely protected them. God is able to take us through the most difficult of trials without us ever being harmed. Whatever the trial you are facing today, the Lord can protect you and keep you through it.

Nebuchadnezzar was so struck by what had happened that day that he praised the God of Shadrach, Meshach, and Abednego. He praised them for their commitment to their God and willingness to face the furnace rather than to dishonor him. Right there that day Nebuchadnezzar made a decree that people of all nations and languages were to respect the God of Israel. Anyone who spoke out against the God of Israel was to be cut in pieces and their home turned into a pile of rubble. Before all those present, he confessed that there was no other god who could save in this way. As for Shadrach, Meshach, and Abednego, they were promoted in authority. God honored their obedience. He will honor all who honor him.

*For Consideration:*

- How does this story challenge you in your commitment to being obedient to the Lord?

- Would you be willing to be obedient even to the point of death?

- Notice here that Daniel's friends chose not to defend themselves. They cast themselves completely on God. Why do we feel that we have to defend ourselves? Does this indicate a lack of faith in God's provision and protection?

- What does this chapter teach us about how God meets us in the struggles we face on a daily basis?

*For Prayer:*

- Thank the Lord for the wonderful way in which he protected his servants in this chapter. Thank him that he is able to protect us in the same way.

- Ask the Lord to give you the faith to be obedient in the struggles that come your way.

- Thank the Lord for the way he meets us in the struggles we face in life.

# 4
# The Humbling of Nebuchadnezzar

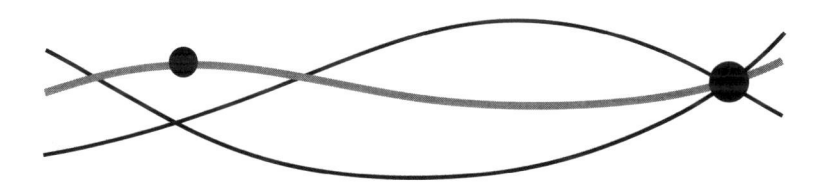

*Read Daniel 4:1–37*

If there is one thing that is certain in the early pages of the book of Daniel, it is that God was speaking to the heart of Nebuchadnezzar. It is quite interesting to see how the Lord revealed himself to this king. God spoke to Nebuchadnezzar in dreams, miracles, and through his servant Daniel. Nebuchadnezzar heard about the God of Israel and was impressed by his power and majesty, yet, up to this point, never surrendered to him as the only Lord. There are many people like this. They have seen God do wonderful things, and they have heard much about him, but they have never given him their hearts and lives.

God was not finished with Nebuchadnezzar. There was a work he wanted to do in this man's life. The work of softening Nebuchadnezzar's heart would not come easy for Nebuchadnezzar, but God would accomplish his purpose in the life of this world ruler. Here in this chapter we have a letter that King Nebuchadnezzar wrote to all people in his empire. Nebuchadnezzar was not someone to do something in a half-hearted way. He wrote to show the world how the Most High God of Israel had dealt with him (verse 2).

Nebuchadnezzar understood that the God of Daniel performed great signs and mighty wonders. He recognized that the kingdom of this God is an eternal kingdom that would have no end. He rules from generation to generation (verse 3). Unlike the rule of Nebuchadnezzar, this God would never die or cease to reign. In saying these things, Nebuchadnezzar confessed that the Lord God of Israel was superior to him and worthy of all praise and worship. This is really quite a remarkable statement from the lips of the most powerful king on the earth.

Nebuchadnezzar recounted the story of how he had been in his palace when he had a dream. Notice in verse 4 that Nebuchadnezzar explained that he was contented and prosperous in his palace. He had everything his heart could want. There was nothing lacking in his life. This particular dream terrified the king, and he called on the wise men of the kingdom to interpret the dream for him (verse 6).

These wise men were brought to the king. Among them were magicians, enchanters, astrologers, and diviners. These were the best spiritualists in the empire, but they could not interpret the king's dream.

When everyone else had failed to interpret this dream, Daniel came into the presence of the king. It appears that he had not been called the first time. We do not know why he had not been summoned earlier with the other wise men.

Nebuchadnezzar had made Daniel chief of the magicians and knew that the spirit of the holy gods was in him (verse 8). He expected great things of Daniel's God. He believed that there was not a mystery that was too difficult for him. The king believed that if anyone could interpret the dream, it would be Daniel. So, Nebuchadnezzar told his dream to Daniel.

Nebuchadnezzar explained that when he was lying in his bed, he saw a tree in the middle of the land. The thing he noticed about this tree was its size. It grew very large and tall, and its top touched the sky (verse 11). It was so big that it could be seen from the ends of the earth. The other thing about this tree was that its leaves were beautiful, and the fruit it produced was so abundant that it could feed everyone on the earth. Under the tree the beasts of the field found shelter. The birds of the air lived in its branches. Every creature on the earth depended on this tree for food.

While Nebuchadnezzar watched in his dream, he saw a holy messenger come down from heaven with a message calling for the tree to be cut down. The branches of the tree were to be trimmed off and its leaves stripped. Its fruit was to be scattered. When this happened, the animals who found shelter under its shade and the birds that rested in its branches were forced to flee.

In his dream the king heard the messenger command that the stump and the roots were to remain in the ground, bound with iron and bronze. All that was left of the once-glorious tree was a stump. The glory had faded, and the tree was left for dead. The stump was drenched with the dew from heaven. It would live among the animals of the earth. Its mind would be changed from the mind of a man to the mind of an animal for the period of "seven times" or seven years (verse 16).

The messenger reminded his listeners that the decision had been made. The verdict had been announced by messenger so that all the earth might know that the Most High God of Israel is the sovereign God of the nations. He gives his kingdoms to whomever he wants and places whomever he chooses over those kingdoms (verse 17).

When Nebuchadnezzar finished explaining to Daniel what he had seen and heard, the king reminded Daniel that none of his magicians could interpret the dream for him. He told Daniel that he had great confidence in him and his ability to interpret this dream for him. He knew this because he recognized that the "spirit of the holy gods" was in him. Nebuchadnezzar spoke from his pagan perspective and not from the perspective of a believer. In reality, Daniel had the presence of the Holy Spirit with him and not the spirit of the gods.

When Daniel heard the king's dream, he was troubled in his heart for some time (verse 19). Nebuchadnezzar noticed that Daniel's thoughts troubled him greatly. Seeing this, Nebuchadnezzar sought to comfort Daniel and asked him to explain the meaning of the dream.

Daniel began by telling the king that he wished that the dream applied to one of his enemies and not to him. This was an indication of the terrible nature of the interpretation of this dream. Daniel said that Nebuchadnezzar was the tree that grew so large and tall. As a powerful king, he was known throughout the entire earth. He prospered greatly, and many people depended on him for their food and livelihood. Many took shelter in his branches and shade.

As for the interpretation of the messenger's words, Daniel told the king that the time was coming when he would be driven away from people to live with wild animals. He would eat grass like cattle and be drenched daily with dew for a period of seven years. After that time he would come to understand that the Most High is sovereign over all kings and kingdoms and gives those kingdoms to anyone he chooses. Nebuchadnezzar was given his kingdom by God—it was not his personal creation. The fact that the messenger commanded that the roots remain was to show Nebuchadnezzar that his kingdom would be restored on the day that he recognized that "Heaven rules" (verse 26). Only when Nebuchadnezzar surrendered to God would he be set free from his bondage.

This was not an easy interpretation for Daniel to announce to the king. Daniel revealed that the king's pride had caused God's judgment. Nebuchadnezzar believed that he was the ruler of the earth. He did not believe that he was subject to the God of Israel, a nation that he had conquered. God would humble him until he recognized that he was nothing without the Lord God. The king would be humbled until he recognized that Israel's God is the God of heaven and earth and that everything the king had came from him.

In verse 27 Daniel pleaded with Nebuchadnezzar to renounce his sin and do what was right. Only if he turned from his sins could these things be avoided. Only if he repented and did what was right could he be restored. Daniel confronted him openly with his sin. He told the king to stop oppressing his people and be kind to them instead. These were bold words from the lips of a captive, especially as they were directed to a king who had shown himself to be severe toward those who displeased him (see 2:12).

It was twelve months later that the king was walking on the roof of his palace in Babylon. He looked out over his kingdom, and his heart swelled in pride. "Is not this the great Babylon I have built as the royal residence, by my mighty power and for the glory of my majesty?" he asked (verse 30).

The words were still on his lips when a voice came down from heaven: "Your royal authority has been taken from you. You will be driven away from people and will live with the wild animals; you will eat grass like cattle. Seven times will pass by for you until you acknowledge that the Most High is sovereign over the kingdoms of men and gives them to anyone he wishes" (verses 31–32).

With those words the prophecy of Daniel was fulfilled. Nebuchadnezzar was driven away from people and ate grass like cattle. His hair grew long like the feathers of an eagle, and his fingernails grew long like the claws of an animal. For a period of seven years, the king lost his mind. There was no glory in living like a maniac with the wild animals. He was shown clearly that, in an instant, he could lose all that he had worked so hard to achieve.

The king's pride was a horrible thing in the eyes of the Lord because he failed to realize that the Lord God of Israel had given him everything he had. He failed to understand that without God he would have nothing. What made this even worse was the fact that the Lord had been revealing himself to King Nebuchadnezzar through Daniel for some time, but the king refused to surrender to him. He had many opportunities to humble himself before the Lord and his purposes but

**The Humbling of Nebuchadnezzar** ● 27

refused to do so. He continued in his pride and arrogance. It was not until the Lord struck him in this way that the king came to realize he was subject to God. At the end of the appointed time that God had set for him, Nebuchadnezzar raised his eyes to heaven and his sanity was restored. God gave him a second chance. God could have completely destroyed him but decided instead to teach him a lesson. There were several things that Nebuchadnezzar learned in this time.

In verse 34 Nebuchadnezzar praised the Most High God and honored him as the God who lives forever and whose kingdom and dominion are eternal. He recognized that the kingdom he had called his own was really the Lord's kingdom. Here we have the most powerful king on the surface of the earth submitting to the Lord and recognizing that the earth is the Lord's. This is a different attitude from the one he had when he made the statement to Shadrach, Meshach, and Abednego in Daniel 3:15: "What god will be able to rescue you from my hand?"

Notice in verse 35 that he realized also that all people of the earth are regarded as nothing to this God. In other words, there is no one who can be compared to the Lord God of Israel. This God does whatever he pleases with the earth. Everything comes from him. No one can hold back God's hand or even question what he does. He is a sovereign and all-powerful God to whom every knee must bow.

Nebuchadnezzar had a change of heart. He realized that the God of Israel is the one true God and that he owed everything to that God. Notice that the moment he came to understand this, his honor was restored to him. He returned to his throne and became even greater than he was before. This time, however, there was a change. Now he praised the King of Heaven and recognized that those who walk in pride God is able to humble. Nebuchadnezzar saw how God hates pride. The lesson he learned over those seven years would not be easily forgotten.

There are several important things we need to understand in this passage. First, we need to see how terrible pride is in God's eyes. Pride places itself in God's place. It boldly proclaims that it does not need God. It was the sin that drove Satan from heaven, and anyone else who falls to it will be led to failure and defeat. What we need to understand here is just how much we are dependent on God for everything. Were it not for him, we would have nothing at all.

There is another important lesson for us to learn here. For Nebuchadnezzar there could be no growth until pride was broken in his life. Only when he recognized and confessed his sin could he be restored to sanity and service. By learning his lesson, new and fresh blessings were poured on him. The same is true for us as well. Only when we learn what God is teaching us can we advance in our spiritual walks. There are obstacles for each of us that need to be overcome before we can move on to greater things.

*For Consideration:*

- What does this chapter teach us about how dependent we are on the Lord?
- What do we learn about the horrible nature of the sin of pride?
- What do we learn about second chances from this chapter?
- What lessons has God been teaching you about pride?

*For Prayer:*

- Thank the Lord that he is a sovereign God who is in control of all things.
- Ask the Lord to expose and break any area of pride in your life.
- Thank the Lord that, as he did for Nebuchadnezzar, he has often shown mercy to you and given you another chance.

- Thank the Lord that while he sometimes disciplines us, he remains in control and takes us through difficulties to teach us what we need to learn.

# 5
# Writing on the Wall

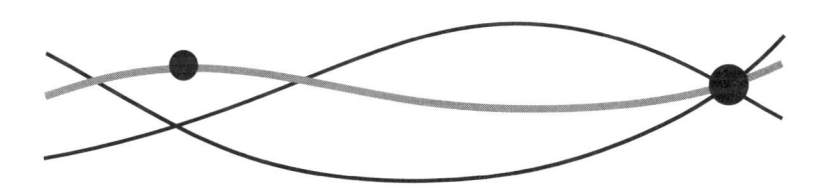

*Read Daniel 5:1–31*

In chapter 5 we move from the life of Nebuchadnezzar to King Belshazzar. Belshazzar was a grandson of Nebuchadnezzar. A certain time had passed here in the story. Belshazzar was the last king of Babylon before it was conquered by the Medes and the Persians. At this time the end of Babylon's glory days had arrived.

Despite the fact that the enemy was pressing hard against him and his kingdom, King Belshazzar decided to hold a great banquet. A thousand nobles were invited to this great feast. In verse 1 we learn that the king drank wine with these nobles. Culturally, the king would have ordinarily drank and eaten apart from the nobles. On this occasion, however, he put aside common etiquette.

While the king and the nobles were drinking wine, Belshazzar gave orders that the gold and silver goblets that his father (actually grandfather) Nebuchadnezzar had taken from the temple in Jerusalem be brought to him. He commanded that wine be served in these goblets to his nobles, his wives, and his concubines. Again, it is important to note here that women were present at this banquet. Historically, the women were kept apart from men at such festivities.

The temple goblets were brought to the king as he commanded, and wine was served from them to those at the feast. As they drank they praised the gods of gold, silver, bronze, iron, wood, and stone (verse 4). Notice the number of gods they praised here. It is important to note that these individuals dishonored the God of Israel by using goblets consecrated to him. Not only did Belshazzar have no concern for the common etiquette of the day, he also had no concern or respect for the God of Israel.

As the people ate and drank, the fingers of a human hand appeared before them and wrote on a plaster wall near a lampstand. Verse 5 tells us that the king watched as the hand wrote on the wall. This would lead us to believe that the message was particularly for him. This is confirmed in verse 6 where Daniel tells us the king's response to the writing. His face turned pale, and he become so frightened that his knees knocked together and his legs gave way. It could be that he passed out or, at least, fell to the floor. He was terrified by what he saw.

King Belshazzar called out for his enchanters, astrologers, and diviners to see if they could make any sense out of the writing on the wall. He told the wise men that the one who was able to interpret this writing would become the third highest ruler in the kingdom. Historically, the first place would have been given to the king. The second place would have been given to the king's son. This person would be clothed in purple as a sign of royalty and dignity and have a gold chain placed around his neck. Despite these promises, the wise men who stood before the king could not understand the writing on the wall. The meaning of the words was hidden from them. This made the king more afraid (verse 9).

Terror and confusion were heard in the voices of the king and his nobles. In verse 10 the queen heard these voices and came into the banquet hall to see what was happening. She sought to comfort the king. She reminded Belshazzar about Daniel and how, in the time of Nebuchadnezzar, he had been found to have wisdom and intelligence that was like the gods. She told Belshazzar how Daniel had been appointed chief of the magicians, enchanters, and astrologers. She was quite confident that Daniel would be able to read the writing and tell Belshazzar its meaning. As in chapters 2 and 4, the wisdom of the world is found to be completely inadequate to solve the world's problems, but God speaks true wisdom to and through his children.

Belshazzar called for Daniel, and he was brought before the king (verse 13). Belshazzar told Daniel how the wise men were not able to explain the writing on the wall. He told Daniel that if he could interpret the writing, he would be clothed in purple, have a gold chain put on his neck, and be the third highest ruler in the kingdom (verse 16). This would lead us to believe that at the death of Nebuchadnezzar, Daniel had lost his position. Belshazzar may have chosen his own officials. Under Nebuchadnezzar, Daniel already had the authority Belshazzar was offering him here.

Daniel was not interested in the king's gifts and told him to keep his gifts for himself and give his rewards to someone else. Daniel was not interested in position and authority, nor was he interested in selling the wisdom God so graciously gave to him.

Daniel explained to the king that the Most High God had given his forefather Nebuchadnezzar great sovereignty, glory, and splendor (verse 18). Daniel reminded Belshazzar, however, that Nebuchadnezzar's heart became proud, and this resulted in him being stripped of his glory and splendor (verse 20). He was driven from people and lived as an animal until the time he willingly acknowledged that the Most High God is completely sovereign over all kingdoms on the earth.

Daniel told Belshazzar that he had not humbled himself but had repeated the same error. Belshazzar had openly defied the Most High God by taking the temple goblets and using them to drink wine for his banquet. With these goblets in his hands, he had praised the gods of gold, silver, bronze, iron, wood, and stone. Daniel told him, "You did not honor the God who holds in his hand your life and all your ways" (verse 23). Because Belshazzar had openly defied the Most High God, the Lord sent the hand that wrote the inscription.

In verse 25 we see that the inscription written on the wall read: "Mene, Mene, Tekel, Parsin." Daniel explained what these words meant. *Mene*, Daniel told the king, means "numbered." This referred to the fact that the days of the Belshazzar's reign were being numbered and coming to an end. *Tekel* means "weighed." Daniel told Belshazzar that he personally had been weighed and found wanting. He did not measure up to the standard that God had laid out for him. *Parsin* or *Peres* means "divided." The kingdom was going to be divided and given to the Medes and the Persians.

True to his word, Belshazzar gave the position of third in command to Daniel. This, of course, did not mean anything because Daniel had just prophesied that the kingdom was going to be taken by the Medes and the Persians. The position was of no value to him or anyone else. That very night Belshazzar was killed, and Darius the Mede took the kingdom by force at the age of sixty-two. The prophecy did not delay in coming to pass.

There are several things that should be examined in greater detail in this chapter. We see how God responded when those things that had been consecrated to him were defiled. He took this matter seriously. Our bodies are the temple of the Holy Spirit and are consecrated to God. It is important that we respect these temples.

Notice second that, as it was for Nebuchadnezzar, Belshazzar fell because of his pride. He did not learn the lesson of his forefather Nebuchadnezzar. We who have read this story and see the result of pride in the lives of Nebuchadnezzar and Belshazzar must learn this lesson well. Pride will destroy us. We are warned in this chapter to flee from pride. God will judge this sin very seriously.

Do you think it is strange that God spoke to Belshazzar in a manner he could not understand? Why did God not simply write these words in an understandable fashion? This would have avoided the need of an interpreter. But the inability to understand the writing on the wall led to Belshazzar knowing that the God of Israel was speaking to him. None of the magicians or enchanters of Babylon could understand the meaning of these words. Only Daniel, the servant of the Most High God of Israel, could understand them. Those present would realize that this mystery could only be solved by the God of Israel. It was he who was speaking to Belshazzar.

*For Consideration:*

- What does this passage teach us about the sin of pride?

- Belshazzar had not learned the lesson God had taught Nebuchadnezzar, even though Nebuchadnezzar had written that lesson down. Why is it so difficult for us to learn the lessons God wants to teach us?

- What does this chapter reveal about respect for God and his ways?

- Why was it significant that only Daniel could interpret the writing on the wall? What did this prove to Belshazzar?

*For Prayer:*

- Ask the Lord to give you a deeper understanding and respect for his majesty and glory.

- Ask the Lord to keep you from the sin of pride.

- Ask the Lord to teach you the lessons he wants you to learn. Ask him to soften your heart so that you can learn these lessons before it is too late.

# 6

# In the Lions' Den

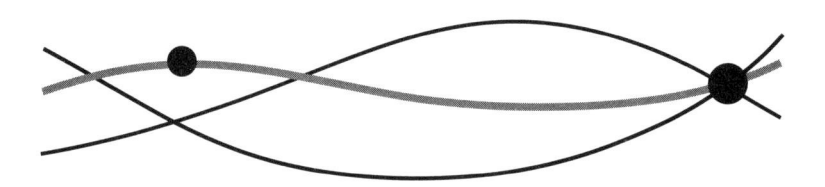

*Read Daniel 6:1–28*

In the last chapter, we saw that King Darius the Mede conquered Babylon. Many historians believe this happened on October 29, 539 BC. Following this victory he decided to set up 120 *satraps* or regional officials throughout the kingdom. Obviously, these officials were accountable to him and carried out his decrees in these regions. Three administrators were given responsibility over these 120 satraps. Daniel was one of the three administrators. This was a very significant role.

Verse 3 tells us that Daniel was so skilled as an administrator that the king planned to place him over the whole kingdom. What we need to understand here is that Daniel was gifted by God with this wisdom for administration. Associated with this gift was the ability to interpret dreams and see the future. Not only did Daniel have the God-given ability to administer but he was also given the gift to be able to see the direction that God wanted to go. We need to see men and women in our day who are able to hear from God and who have the skills necessary to carry those plans through to completion.

Not everyone was pleased with Daniel's authority. Satan was successful in riling certain satraps and administrators against Daniel. These individuals sought to find grounds to lay charges against Daniel in the way he conducted the affairs of the government. However, they were unable to find any fault with him in this matter. In all things Daniel proved to be completely trustworthy and faithful. They could find neither corruption in him nor any areas of his work where he was being negligent. This is a real example for us in our own work and ministry.

Frustrated in their search, these men decided that they would not find anything against Daniel unless it was something to do with his God (verse 5). Knowing that Daniel was a man of God, they determined that they would seek a way to discredit him before the king in regard to his faith.

In verse 6 the administrators and the satraps went to the king and told him that they had decided to honor him by suggesting that for a period of thirty days, no one was to pray to any god except the king. If any one prayed to another god, they were to be thrown into a lions' den. They did this under the guise of showing their devotion to the king, but it actually was a plot of jealousy against Daniel. In verse 8 they asked the king to issue a decree by putting this law in writing and sealing it so that it could not be repealed. The king agreed with them and put the law in writing. A Medo-Persian law could not be changed even by the king.

When Daniel learned of the decree, he went upstairs in his room where the windows faced Jerusalem, got on his knees, and prayed as was his custom (verse 10). He refused to stop praying to his God. He refused even to pray in secret. Daniel prayed openly where all could see him, as he had always done. He did not fear what the satraps and administrators would do to him. And with such terrible evil at his doorstep and in the hearts of the government officials, this kingdom needed Daniel's prayers.

This was the activity that the administrators and the satraps were waiting for. They found Daniel praying and "asking God for help" (verse 11). While the passage does not clearly tell us why he was asking for help, we can be relatively sure that it related to the present situation and the decree of the king. We find in this verse the secret to the success Daniel had been experiencing: he brought all matters to the Lord. He saw it as part of his duty to spend three times a day praying and seeking God's wisdom and blessing on his work and ministry.

Having found Daniel praying, the administrators and satraps went to the king and told him what had happened. They informed him that Daniel did not acknowledge the decree of the king but continued to pray three times a day to the God of Israel. When the king heard this, he was greatly distressed and determined to rescue Daniel (verse 14). This shows us the respect he had for Daniel. Darius tried until sundown to find a way of rescuing Daniel from the consequences of the new law. The administrators and satraps continued to pressure the king to throw Daniel into the lions' den. They reminded him that the law could not be changed. The king was forced to give the order that Daniel be thrown into the lions' den. As they threw Daniel into the pit, the king said to him: "May your God, whom you serve continually, rescue you" (verse 16). The king had a deep respect for Daniel not only because of his work but also because of his tremendous faith.

A stone was brought and placed over the mouth of the den. The king sealed it with his own signet ring so that it could not be opened. The nobles also placed the mark of their rings on the den to show their support of the king's decision. No one would dare to touch that stone on pain of death.

That night the king did not sleep. He refused to eat and spent the night without any entertainment being brought to him. His heart was broken by what he had done. At the first light of day, the king got up and hurried to the lions' den. This act indicated that he may have believed it was possible that the God of Israel would rescue Daniel from these lions. He hoped that this was the case. When he approached the den, he called out to Daniel: "Has your God, whom you serve continually, been able to rescue you from the lions?" (verse 20).

From the den the voice of Daniel replied: "O king, live forever! My God sent his angel, and he shut the mouths of the lions. They have not hurt me, because I was found innocent in his sight. Nor have I ever done any wrong before you, O king" (verses 21–22). Daniel was protected by the sovereign power of God. God's angel protected him all night long. We can only imagine what it was like for Daniel to know the presence and fellowship of that angel with those hungry lions all around him.

Notice the response of the king in verse 23. He was overjoyed. He ordered that Daniel be taken out of the den. There was not even a scratch on him. Notice that the reason for this was because he trusted in the Lord. That trust came when he willingly persisted in praying despite the command of the king. It was his trust in the Lord that kept the mouths of the lions closed. God honored him because he honored God.

When Daniel was brought out of the den, the king commanded that the men who had plotted against him be thrown into the den, along with their wives and children. Verse 24 tells us that before their bodies reached the floor of the den, the lions overpowered them and crushed their bones. This demonstrated to all present that Daniel was truly protected by God and was his servant.

After this incident King Darius wrote to all people, languages, and nations in his kingdom. In this letter he issued a decree that people were to fear the God of Daniel. He publicly declared that the God of Daniel was the living God whose kingdom would never be destroyed. This phrase reminds us of the dream of Nebuchadnezzar that told of a kingdom made without human hands that would endure forever (see 2:44–45). The God of Daniel would reign forever. "For he is the living God and he endures forever; his kingdom will not be destroyed, his dominion will never end. He rescues and he saves; he performs signs and wonders in the heavens and on the earth" (verses 26–27). He rescued Daniel from the mouths of the lions and proved that he is God of all. This sign from God seems to have had a powerful impact on Darius. Verse 28 tells us that Daniel prospered during the reigns of both Darius and Cyrus of Persia. His faithfulness to God brought tremendous blessing on him and the nations he served.

*For Consideration:*

- What is the connection between Daniel's faithfulness to the Lord and his enemies' desire to attack him?

- Take a moment to consider your own life. Have you been faithful and trustworthy? Does the Lord need to do some work on you in any particular area of your life?

- Would you have the boldness of Daniel to stand firm if a similar situation took place in your life?

- What does this passage teach us about the protection of the Lord on the lives of his servants?

*For Prayer:*

- Ask the Lord to give us more leaders like Daniel in our governments and churches.

- Ask the Lord to give you a heart to pray like Daniel for the wisdom and guidance necessary for your ministry.

- Thank the Lord that he is faithful and will protect and keep us in his purposes.

- Ask God to give you the boldness and faithfulness of Daniel.

# 7

# The Four Beasts

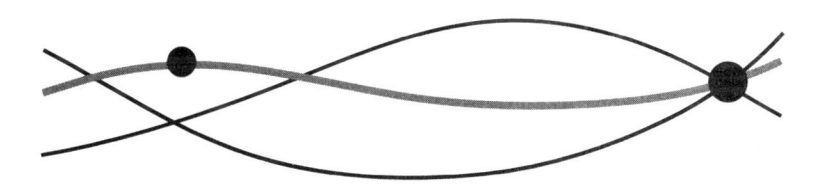

*Read Daniel 7:1–28*

Throughout history God has used many different ways to speak to his people. In the case of Daniel, God used prophetic dreams and visions and also gave Daniel a particular gift to interpret them. The dreams and visions that Daniel had were very complicated and needed much interpretation. Through these revelations the Lord taught him about the things that would come to pass.

The first of these visions is recorded in chapter 7. Daniel received this vision in the first year of Belshazzar, king of Babylon. This places chapter 7 before chapters 5 and 6 in time, as chapter 6 recounts the story of Belshazzar's death.

In his vision Daniel saw the winds of heaven churning up a great sea. The winds of the north, south, east, and west were all causing a great turmoil on the sea. The sea possibly represents the nations of the world. It is important to note that these winds were from heaven. This would indicate that they were some form of judgment on the earth. These winds seemed to act against each other. As they blew from different directions, the sea was being tossed with great violence. Daniel saw four different beasts come up from the turbulent sea. It was as if these beasts had been buried in the depths of the sea, and the winds had aroused them, releasing them from their prison. What is important for us to understand is that these beasts were released as a result of the winds from heaven. In other words, it was the sovereign plan and purpose of God to release them. You can be assured that the Lord always remains in complete control of what is happening on this earth.

Each of the beasts was different in appearance. The first beast was like a lion but had the wings of an eagle. The wings of this lion were torn off, and it was standing on its two back feet. It was also given the heart of a man. Who is this lion and what does it represent?

There are several important details that we need to understand about this vision before we continue. Many commentators see a similarity between the dream that Nebuchadnezzar had of the great statue in chapter 2 and Daniel's vision in chapter 7. In the dream of chapter 2, Nebuchadnezzar saw a statue with four parts: a gold head, a silver chest and arms, a bronze belly and thighs, and iron legs and feet. In the vision of chapter 7, Daniel saw four beasts. This similarity cannot go unnoticed. In chapter 2 Daniel explained that the gold head of the statue was King Nebuchadnezzar. It seems quite clear that the first beast that came out of the sea in this vision represents Nebuchadnezzar. There are several reasons for this.

The lion represents the king of the beasts. The eagle is a very majestic bird and can be thought of as the king of the birds. Nebuchadnezzar was a very powerful ruler in his day. The nations of the earth were subject to him. Notice in verse 4 that the wings of the lion were torn off. This great lion, in some way, experienced a great humbling. Nebuchadnezzar clearly experienced this humbling when his pride led to the judgment of God in his life. His sanity was taken from him, and he was stripped of his "wings" and left to live with the animals of the field. Notice in verse 4, however, that after the tearing off of its wings, the lion was lifted up on two feet and given the heart of a man. This is exactly what happened to Nebuchadnezzar. When the time of his judgment was over, he was given back his sanity. He returned to living among humans and was restored to power and authority, though he never had the power he once knew.

The second beast Daniel saw looked like a bear (verse 5). The bear is not as majestic as the lion but still very powerful. This second beast may correspond to the second kingdom of chapter 2, represented by the chest and arms made of silver. Notice that the bear rose up on one of its sides and had three ribs in its mouth. The fact that these ribs were between the teeth of this bear is significant. It indicates that whomever the ribs belonged to had been conquered by the bear. Many commentators see the bear as the nation of the Medes and the Persians, with the stronger side being the Persians. If this is the case, then the ribs are the kingdoms that the Medes and the Persians conquered: Egypt, Lydia, and Babylonia. This bear was told to rise and eat its fill of flesh. Medo-Persia was a very cruel kingdom and conquered and destroyed many nations.

In verse 6 Daniel saw a third beast rising from the sea. This beast was like a leopard. It had four wings on its back, like a bird. It also had four heads and was given authority to rule. It is generally believed that this leopard, which was not quite as majestic as the lion, represents the nation of Greece under Alexander the Great, who conquered the Medo-Persian Empire to become the next great world power. It is important to note, historically, that after the death of Alexander the Great, his kingdom was divided into four parts (323 BC). The regions of Macedon and Greece were handed to a ruler by the name of Cassander. Thrace and Bithynia were led by Lysimachus. Ptolemy governed the region of Egypt. Finally, Seleucus was given authority over the region of Asia and Palestine. These four heads on the leopard may very well represent these four leaders who were given authority to rule over the Greek Empire following the death of Alexander the Great.

The fourth beast was the most terrifying of all the beasts. It had large iron teeth and crushed, devoured, and trampled its victims underfoot. This beast was different from the others, and Daniel noticed that it had ten horns (verse 7). As he looked at these horns, he saw a little horn grow out, uprooting three of the first horns. The little horn spoke boastfully.

There are many similarities between the fourth nation of Nebuchadnezzar's dream of the statue in chapter 2 and this fourth beast. Let's consider them here. Daniel 2:40–41 says this: "Finally, there will be a fourth kingdom, strong as iron—for iron breaks and smashes everything—and as iron breaks things to pieces, so it will crush and break all the others. Just as you saw that the feet and toes were partly of baked clay and partly of iron, so this will be a divided kingdom; yet it will have some of the strength of iron in it, even as you saw iron mixed with clay."

Notice here that this fourth kingdom in Nebuchadnezzar's statue in chapter 2 was a kingdom of iron. Daniel's beast in chapter 7 had teeth of iron. In Nebuchadnezzar's dream this fourth kingdom would smash and break many nations. This is what Daniel saw in his vision here in chapter 7. This fourth beast would trample and devour. More than the other kingdoms, this kingdom would be very violent. This seemed to strike fear in the heart of Daniel.

This fourth beast was not clearly described. It is generally understood to represent Rome, which was the next great world power after Greece. It is interesting to note that Daniel saw 10 horns on this beast, representing different leaders of this great empire. The feet of Nebuchadnezzar's statue had ten toes, possibly representing these same leaders as the ten horns on the beast of Daniel's vision. It is quite difficult to speculate as to the identity of these ten leaders. It seems even more difficult to speculate as to the exact identity of the small horn that boasted. Opinions range from the Antichrist who is to come to a variety of historical figures in the history of Rome.

After the fourth beast, Daniel saw thrones being set in

place. As he watched, the "Ancient of Days" took his place (verse 9). Daniel described him as being clothed in white with hair as white as wool. The color white is a symbol of purity. This being was absolutely pure. He sat on a throne that was a flaming fire. There were blazing wheels on this throne. The fire may very well represent the holiness of this being who sat on the throne. He was surrounded by holy fire. The term "Ancient of Days" can really only be applied to God himself and particularly to God the Father in this chapter.

In verse 10 Daniel saw a river of fire flowing out from the Ancient of Days who sat on the throne. This river of fire could represent a purifying and judging fire that flowed throughout the world. The Ancient of Days was surrounded by thousands and thousands of people who served him. Beyond this there were millions of people who stood before him. The scene is like that of a courtroom. Books were opened before the Ancient of Days as he sat on his throne.

As Daniel watched he heard the boastful horn utter terrible words. This horn was not threatened by what was happening before him. Daniel watched until the beast with the ten horns was slain and its body destroyed by blazing fire. God's judgment fell first on the nation that had been such a terror to the earth. Rome would fall and be destroyed. That little horn resisted to the end with its boasting and blasphemous words but was eventually destroyed and cast into the fire of God's judgment. This image is similar to the stone smashing the toes of the statue in chapter 2. As for the first three beasts, they were stripped of their authority but allowed to live for a time (verse 12). This corresponds to the idea that each world empire survived in the succeeding empires through its descendants. However, God's judgment would completely destroy the final world kingdom, because Christ's kingdom would replace it.

In verse 13 Daniel told his readers that as he watched he saw one like a son of man coming in the clouds of heaven. The son of man approached the Ancient of Days and was given great authority, glory, and power over all people. People of every language worshiped him, and he set up an everlasting kingdom that would never be destroyed. Again, it is interesting to compare Nebuchadnezzar's dream in chapter 2 with the vision of chapter 7. In chapter 2 a great rock was formed with hands that were not human. That rock came and crushed the statue. The rock represented an eternal kingdom, not made with human hands, that would never be destroyed (see 2:44–45). In a similar way, in chapter 7 the son of man was seen setting up his kingdom. It would be a kingdom that would never be destroyed. The Lord Jesus, the Son of Man, would receive this glorious kingdom as a reward from his Father for his earthly life of obedience and his atoning work on the cross. (See Philippians 2:5–11. Elsewhere in Scripture the eternal kingdom is presented as both earthly and heavenly—see Isaiah 11 as well as Revelation 21 and 22. Commentators differ in their understanding of the phases of the eternal kingdom.)

As Daniel watched this vision unfold before him, he was troubled in his spirit. In verse 16 he told his readers that in his vision he approached "one of those standing there" and asked him to explain the meaning of the vision. It is unclear who Daniel was speaking about here. It may be that he spoke to one of the individuals gathered around the fiery throne of God. It may have been an angel of God.

The interpreter gave Daniel a very basic understanding of the vision. He told Daniel that the four beasts were four kingdoms that would rise from the earth. We have already said that they probably represent the world empires of Babylon, Medo-Persia, Greece, and Rome. The kingdom set up by the son of man, however, would be a kingdom that the saints of the Most High God would receive. This kingdom would last forever (verse 18).

Daniel was concerned about the fourth beast and what that beast represented. This beast was particularly troubling for Daniel. If this fourth beast represented Rome, it is understandable why Daniel would be so troubled by it. Under this kingdom many believers would be killed.

Historically, in the Roman Empire those who called themselves Christians would be cast to the lions and devoured as sport for the entertainment of the Roman emperors. It is said that one such emperor used the burning bodies of Christians to light his gardens. It would be the Romans who would crucify the Lord Jesus. Could it be that Daniel was sensing some of these terrible tragedies in this vision? It is clear that he understood that this empire would crush and devour many victims (verse 19).

Daniel also asked for an explanation of the ten horns and the other horn that grew up, whose mouth spoke with terrible boasting. This boasting horn troubled him because he saw it waging war on the saints and defeating many of them (verse 21). Daniel saw this in his vision. This terrible persecution continued until the Ancient of Days came and pronounced judgment on this nation and established his own kingdom.

Daniel's interpreter told him that the fourth beast was a nation that would do tremendous damage to the earth. The ten horns were kings of that kingdom that would arise (verse 24). After those ten kings, another king would arise who was different from them. He would subdue three kings and speak out boldly against the Most High God. In particular, he would oppress the saints. During this time the saints would be handed over to him for "a time, times and a half time." Many commentators believe that the term *a time* represents one year, and *times* represents two years. If this is the case, the saints would be handed over to this evil tyrant for a period of three and a half years. At the end of that time, the court of heaven would sit, and power would be taken from this oppressor. When that took place, all the kingdoms of the whole earth would be handed over to the saints of the Most High God. His kingdom would be established, and all rulers would worship and obey him (verse 27).

The interpreter's explanation of the fourth beast leaves us still somewhat confused. There is an element of this vision that has already come to pass in the coming of the Lord Jesus to establish his spiritual kingdom in the hearts of his people. There is also an element of this vision that seems to have been accomplished in the Roman Empire with its intense persecution of Christians and its ultimate downfall. There is, however, another aspect to this fourth beast that does not yet seem to have been fulfilled.

There are many similarities between what Daniel saw in his vision and what the apostle John saw in the book of Revelation. Like the vision of Daniel, John saw a beast with ten horns that spoke blasphemies and was allowed to persecute believers for a time:

> Then the angel carried me away in the Spirit into a desert. There I saw a woman sitting on a scarlet beast that was covered with blasphemous names and had seven heads and ten horns. The woman was dressed in purple and scarlet, and was glittering with gold, precious stones and pearls. She held a golden cup in her hand, filled with abominable things and the filth of her adulteries. This title was written on her forehead:
>
> MYSTERY
> BABYLON THE GREAT
> THE MOTHER OF PROSTITUTES
> AND OF THE ABOMINATIONS OF THE
> EARTH.
>
> I saw that the woman was drunk with the blood of the saints, the blood of those who bore testimony to Jesus. (Revelation 17:3–6)

The apostle John also spoke about a period of three and a half years of persecution in Revelation 11:1–2: "I was given a reed like a measuring rod and was told, 'Go and measure the temple of God and the altar, and count the worshipers there. But exclude the outer court; do not measure it, because it has been given to the Gentiles. They will trample on the holy city for 42 months.'"

Forty-two months is equal to three and a half years. John told his readers that for a period of three and a half years, Gentiles would trample the holy city. This same thought is repeated in Revelation 13:5–7: "The beast was given a mouth to utter proud words and blasphemies and to exercise his authority for forty-two months. He opened his mouth to blaspheme God, and to slander his name and his dwelling place and those who live in heaven. He was given power to make war against the saints and to conquer them. And he was given authority over every tribe, people, language and nation."

This Revelation passage is even more specific. John spoke like Daniel of a beast who would blaspheme the Lord God and persecute believers for forty-two months or three and a half years. These similarities cannot be ignored. While some of Daniel's prophecy may have been fulfilled, there seems yet to be a future fulfillment of this prophecy. We will yet see a major persecution of the church in the days of the end. This persecution will be short-lived and measured by God. Daniel reminded his readers in verse 13 that he did see the Son of Man coming in the clouds to deal with the enemy once and for all. While we will yet have to face difficult days as believers, we can be assured of one thing—God is in control. He will win the battle.

Chapter 7 concludes by reminding its readers that when Daniel saw this vision, he was deeply troubled in his spirit. His face was pale from fear and terror at what was going to happen. For some time he kept this vision to himself and did not share it with anyone.

*For Consideration:*

- What does this chapter teach us about the control of God over world affairs?

- This chapter seems to tell us that the days of the end will be trying days. Would you be ready to face these days?

- Daniel described in some detail here the world powers that would come into being in the years that followed his death. What comfort do you take in the fact that God knows all that is going to come to pass?

*For Prayer:*

- Thank the Lord that he does reveal things to his servants so that they can be ready to face what God has planned.

- Ask the Lord to strengthen you to face any persecution that you may personally face.

- Thank the Lord that he already knows the end. Praise him that he is an all-knowing and all-powerful God.

# 8
# The Ram and the Goat

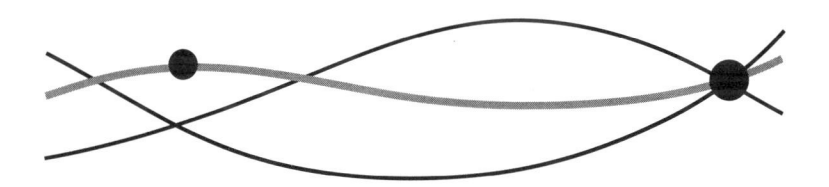

*Read Daniel 8:1–27*

We have in chapter 8 the second recorded vision of the prophet Daniel. This vision occurred in the third year of Belshazzar, king of Babylon. This was two years after the one recorded in chapter 7.

In this second recorded vision, Daniel saw himself in the royal palace of Susa in the province of Elam. Susa was a major city of the Medo-Persian Empire and was located about 250 miles (400 kilometers) east of Babylon (see Esther 1:2; Nehemiah 1:1). Daniel saw himself by the Ulai Canal.

In his vision Daniel saw a ram with two horns, representing power. The ram was standing beside the canal. Daniel noticed that one of the ram's horns was longer than the other. The shorter horn would later grow. We discover in verse 20 that the ram represented the empire of the Medes and the Persians. One horn very likely represented the Medes and the other, the Persians. Commentators believe that the shorter horn represented the Persians who would increase in power in the later part of this empire under Cyrus.

Daniel watched the ram as it charged toward the west, the north, and the south. As the ram charged, no animal could stand in its way. No one could rescue those it conquered. The ram did whatever it pleased and became a great power on the earth. Historically, this was what the Medes and the Persians did. Particularly under Cyrus, this empire expanded its borders by conquest to the west, north, and south (see Isaiah 45:1–7, which was prophesied some 150 years earlier).

In verse 5 Daniel told his readers that in the vision he saw a goat with a very prominent horn between its eyes. This goat came from the west and crossed the whole earth without touching the ground. It was as if this goat was being carried by some external force. In this case, we can assume that this was the power of the Lord who was working out his purposes on the earth. This goat approached the two-horned ram by the canal and charged at it with great rage. Daniel saw the goat attack the ram and strike and shatter its horns. The ram with the two horns was powerless against the attack and was knocked to the ground where it was trampled. We understand that this goat was the nation of Greece, the next great world power. Historians tell us that under Alexander the Great the Greeks attacked and quickly defeated the empire of the Medes and the Persians around 334 BC.

Daniel told his readers in verse 8 that the goat became very great, but at the height of power, its large horn was broken off and replaced by four other horns. Historically, at the height of his power, Alexander the Great died suddenly, and his kingdom was divided into four parts. Seleucus was given the eastern parts of the kingdom; Cassander governed the western regions; Ptolemy ruled in the south; and Lysimachus governed the northern areas. This appears to have been what Daniel saw in his vision. It is quite amazing how God revealed the details of these events to Daniel well before they came to pass.

Out of these four horns came another horn that started out very small but grew in power to the south, east, and toward the "Beautiful Land" (verse 9). This horn continued to grow until it reached the heavens. As Daniel watched, this little horn threw some of the stars down to the earth and trampled on them. It set itself up to be as great as the "Prince of the host," and took away the daily sacrifice from him. The sanctuary of the Prince of the host was brought low under this horn. Many saints were given over to this horn, and it prospered over them. During those days truth was thrown to the ground (verse 12).

Again, it is important to examine what happened historically in order to interpret this prophecy. This little horn came from the Grecian goat. It is clearly identified with Greece. Historically, Greece produced a ruler by the name of Antiochus Epiphanes. He wanted to see the worship of Zeus established in his kingdom. He sought to establish this worship in Jerusalem as well. It is said that Antiochus Epiphanes identified himself with Zeus, the lord of all Greek gods, and wanted to make worship of himself universal throughout his kingdom. It appears that he became so crazed in this effort that he was called *Epimanes* ("madman") instead of *Epiphanes*. He was the first of all the world leaders to actually seek to root out the worship of Jehovah in Jerusalem. It is said that he became so enraged at the Jewish population that he sought to destroy them as a nation. He was successful in trampling on the people of God and took away the worship of Jehovah for a period of three and a half years. It is quite easy to see that this particular Greek ruler could be the initial fulfillment of Daniel's prophecy.

As Daniel watched what was happening in his vision, he heard a voice of a holy one speaking to another holy one (possibly angels). One asked the other how long it would take for the vision to be fulfilled (verse 13). The other holy one told him that it would take 2300 evenings and mornings before the sanctuary would be reconsecrated after being desecrated by this terrible leader. However we interpret these 2300 days, what is important for us to note here is that this time of trampling would not go on forever. The Lord would step in and restore his people. God will not hand his people over to the enemy forever. He will not forget his own.

As Daniel watched this vision unfold, he saw someone standing before him who looked like a man. He listened and heard a voice from the Ulai Canal. The voice cried out: "Gabriel, tell this man the meaning of the vision" (verse 16). The angel Gabriel announced both the birth of John the Baptist and the birth of the Lord Jesus (Luke 1:19, 26). As Gabriel approached, Daniel was terrified and appears to have fainted. Obviously, there was something very majestic about his presence. Gabriel announced that he had come to tell Daniel the meaning of the vision. As Gabriel spoke he touched Daniel and raised him to his feet. It could be that he was trying to express that he was not to be worshiped because he was merely an angel. Daniel stood before him instead of bowing down before him.

Gabriel told Daniel that the vision he had received concerned the time that was to come, "the appointed time of the end" (verse 19). He told Daniel clearly that the two-horned ram represented the kings of Media and Persia (verse 20). The goat that attacked this ram was Greece. The horn between its eyes was their first king. The four horns that replaced the larger one were four kingdoms that would emerge from the nation of Greece. They would not have the same power as the first. In the latter part of their reigns, when rebellion and wickedness had matured in the land, a "stern-faced king" would arise. This king would become very powerful and strong and would succeed in causing terrible devastation. He would destroy mighty men and the holy people. We already spoke of him as Antiochus Epiphanes.

Gabriel told Daniel that this terrible leader would consider himself superior to all others. In the case of Antiochus Epiphanes, he believed himself to be a god. This great king would even take a stand against the Prince of princes, God himself. Gabriel told Daniel, however, that he would die an unnatural death. He would be killed but not by human hands. Historically, Antiochus Epiphanes died when he was on his way to Judea to seek revenge on God's people. His death was terrible—he died as a result of an infestation of worms and ulcers.

Many commentators see a parallel between Antiochus Epiphanes and another fierce leader predicted in New Testament passages (Matthew 24:15–24; 2 Thessalonians 2:3–12; Revelation 13:1–10). Therefore, many believe that this passage in Daniel has a double fulfillment—one in Antiochus Epiphanes and one in the Antichrist who is yet to come.

On seeing this vision, Daniel was exhausted and lay ill for several days. He found the vision very difficult to understand. Why would God allow such terrible things to happen to his people? Gabriel told him that this vision was for the distant future and to seal it up (verse 26). This did not necessarily mean to shut it up to secrecy but to preserve its truth.

There is a very clear sense here that there would still be difficult days coming for the people of God. For a time they would be handed over to their enemies. Many would lose their lives, and persecution would break out in the land.

This was true of the land of Israel under Grecian domination and later Roman domination, and it will also be true for the saints in the days of the end of time. The apostle John saw into the future and prophesied that the day would come when a beast would be given authority over the saints for a time (Revelation 13:7). Like Antiochus Epiphanes, he would call all the inhabitants of the earth to worship him. Many would lose their lives because they would not bow the knee.

There are times to come when being a believer will be enough to bring a sentence of death. Will you be ready to face this level of persecution? Many of our brothers and sisters are already facing this kind of oppression. Daniel prophesied that a terrible ruler would wage war on the saints during Old Testament times. The apostle John foresaw the same thing for those living in New Testament times. May God give us the courage and devotion to him to be able to persevere to the end and be faithful to him when persecution comes our way.

*For Consideration:*

- Are you ready to face the level of persecution that this chapter in Daniel describes?

- What encouragement do you receive from this chapter realizing that God already knows how things on this earth will unfold?

- What do we learn here about God's control over all the politics of Daniel's day?

*For Prayer:*

- Ask the Lord to give you strength to face the opposition that you are facing even now in your life.

- Ask the Lord to raise up a people who are not afraid to suffer for him.

- Thank the Lord that he is a sovereign God who rules over all.

# 9
# Daniel's Prayer

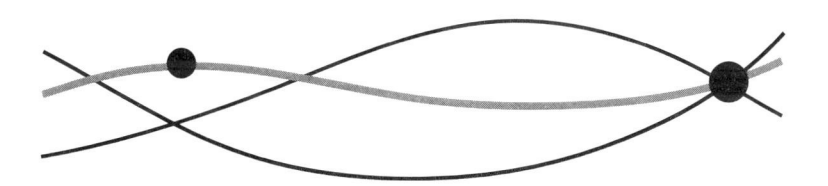

*Read Daniel 9:1–27*

Many years had past since the capture and exile of the people of God to Babylon. At the death of the Babylonian king Belshazzar, Darius the Mede was given the territory of Babylon to rule as viceroy. The time of this chapter is the first year of Darius, placing the date around 537 BC. This would also place the time of this chapter very close to the declaration of Cyrus that allowed the Jews to return home to Israel after 70 years of exile.

It was in this first year of Darius that Daniel was reading his Scriptures and discovered that Jeremiah the prophet had prophesied that the desolation (exile) of Jerusalem would last for seventy years (Jeremiah 25:8–12; 29:10). Daniel realized that this meant that the Israelite exile would end very shortly. We can only imagine how excited Daniel must have been at this discovery. It almost appears that this truth had been hidden from him until the appropriate time.

Notice Daniel's response to this prophecy. In verse 3 Daniel went to the Lord and pleaded with him in prayer and fasting.

He put ashes on himself and dressed in sackcloth. Notice what Daniel prayed. He recognized that God is awesome and keeps his covenant of love with all who love and obey him (verse 4). He confessed that his people had done wrong and rebelled against their God by refusing to obey his commands. God's people had refused to listen to the prophets who had been sent to warn them of the consequences of their ongoing rebellion (verse 6).

In verse 7 Daniel recognized that the Lord had scattered Israel throughout the nations because of sin and rebellion. Israel was in shame. Daniel approached God, whom he knew to be merciful and forgiving (verse 9). The people of Israel deserved the punishment they had received because they had turned from God and his ways. They had been warned by Moses that if they turned from the law of the Lord, then his curse would fall on them (Deuteronomy 28:15–46). The words spoken by Moses had come to pass in Daniel's day. All of Israel and Judah were under that curse. Their rebellion and disobedience had caused the loss of everything they had. The blessing of God was stripped from them. Because they turned away from his law, the Lord brought terrible disaster on them as a people.

Daniel recognized that his people were suffering the consequences of their sins. He confessed the sins of his people to God. Having done this, Daniel reminded the Lord of how he had brought his people out of Egypt and made a name for himself. In verse 16 Daniel pleaded with God to turn his anger and wrath from Jerusalem. He petitioned God to look down in favor on his people for his own name's sake. He cried out for the city of Jerusalem. He asked God to see its desolation and have pity on it.

Daniel was not making this request because God's people were righteous and deserving of this favor from God (verse 18). The fact was that the Israelites in exile in Babylon had the same hearts as their ancestors. Daniel did not come to God on the basis of Israel's righteousness but rather on the basis of God's great mercy.

This is a very powerful insight and one that we all need to understand. How often have we failed to make requests of God because we did not feel worthy? How often have we hesitated to ask for greater things of God because we did not feel that we were spiritual enough to merit such things? Are we not guilty of coming to God on the basis of our self-righteousness and not on the basis of his mercy?

Daniel understood what we need to understand. None of us can come to God on the basis of our righteousness. Every single one of us must come to him on the basis of his mercy to ask for those things we do not deserve. Daniel came boldly to ask God for mercy and favor that was undeserved.

In his prayer Daniel asked the Lord to act for the sake of his name (verses 18–19). He pleaded with God not to delay answering for the sake of the city that bore his name. In reality, he was asking that the prophecy of Jeremiah be accomplished as the Lord had promised. He pleaded with God for the rebuilding and reestablishment of the great city of Jerusalem.

What we need to understand here is that the faith of Daniel was stirred by the word of God that he read in the prophecy of Jeremiah. This stirring up of faith caused him to plead with God in prayer and fasting. Before God caused his people to return to their homeland, he stirred up Daniel to pray. God seems to begin many of his powerful works after human prayer. It is absolutely amazing to see how when Cyrus came to power less than a year after Daniel began to pray, he opened the door for the people of God to return to their homeland. Cyrus also restored the temple furnishings and paid much of the expenses out of his own pocket (Ezra 1). We might say that this was the direct result of Daniel's prayer in this chapter.

As Daniel prayed for Jerusalem and confessed his sin and the sin of his people, the angel Gabriel appeared to him (verse 21). Gabriel came to give him insight and understanding. He told Daniel in verse 23 that as soon as he began to pray, an answer was given. Daniel was still praying, but the answer had already come.

Gabriel was sent with a message to Daniel about future events for God's people. He told Daniel that "seventy 'sevens'" were decreed for the Jews and Jerusalem to atone for their sin and bring in everlasting righteousness (verse 24). This period of seventy sevens would fulfill God's plan for the earth and anoint the most holy. Commentators generally agree here that the seventy sevens represent a period of four hundred and ninety years (seventy times seven). Daniel was told that within this period of time, the sins of God's people would be atoned, prophecy would be accomplished, and everlasting righteousness established on the earth. Within this period of time, God would send his Son to the earth. The Lord Jesus was the one who would atone for the sins of his people. He would fulfill all the prophecies about the Messiah and bring an everlasting righteousness.

In verses 25–27 Gabriel explained to Daniel that from the issuing of the decree to restore and rebuild Jerusalem to the coming of the Anointed One, there would be seven sevens and sixty-two sevens, a total of sixty-nine sevens, or 483 years. Gabriel went on to describe various things that would happen during this period. The first seven sevens (or forty-nine years) represented a time when the temple would be rebuilt.

In the next period of the sixty-two sevens (434 years), the city of Jerusalem would be inhabited. Gabriel told Daniel that times in this rebuilt city would be times of trouble (verse 25). Historically, in the years following the rebuilding of the city and temple, there were cycles of intense persecution of the Jews under Greece and then Rome.

Gabriel told Daniel in verse 26 that after these times were completed, the Anointed One (the Lord Jesus) would be killed, and it would appear that the Anointed One had accomplished nothing. Historically, this is what the disciples thought when the Lord Jesus died. They failed to understand the significance of what he had accomplished in his death. In the years following the death of the Messiah, a ruler would come who would destroy both the temple and the city of Jerusalem. Historically,

Jerusalem was destroyed around 70 AD. War and desolations were decreed for the Jewish nation until the end. We have certainly seen this in the history of the Jewish nation.

In verse 27 Gabriel told Daniel about a final set of seven. This final seven years would take place after the death of the Messiah. During that time a leader would arise who would make a covenant with God's people but would break that covenant and put an end to sacrifice and offering in the temple. He would also set up an abomination in the temple (verse 27). There would be desolations from that period until God brought it to an end.

Historically, by the year 70 AD Rome had completely destroyed the temple in Jerusalem. While the evil ruler that lead this persecution against the Jews would accomplish much evil, he would be held accountable by God and judged for his evil deeds. There are many believers who think this final seven refers to a time yet future and to the Antichrist, or beast, of Revelation 13.

Difficult times were coming for God's people. The Messiah who was promised would die. Jerusalem would again be destroyed. The temple would be ravaged. Daniel was told in advance how all these things would happen so that when they did happen, his people would know that God was in control.

*For Consideration:*

- What does this chapter teach us about how God calls people to pray when he wants to do a mighty work?

- What connection was there between Daniel's prayer and the ease in which the people of God returned to their homeland under Cyrus?

- What do you think God's people learned in their time of exile? What was in their future? Do we learn from the discipline of the Lord in our lives?

- What encouragement do you find in the fact that God described very particularly all the events that would take place up to the days of the Messiah? What does this teach us about God?

*For Prayer:*

- Ask the Lord to enable you to be sensitive to the times he is calling you to pray.

- Thank the Lord that we can come to him on the basis of his mercy. Thank him that we do not have to come to him on the basis of our own righteousness.

- Ask the Lord to give you strength to face the persecution and opposition that may come your way because you are a believer.

- Thank the Lord that he is in control of the future.

- Ask the Lord to teach you the lessons you need to learn so that you do not fall back into the same sins.

# 10

# Michael and the Persians

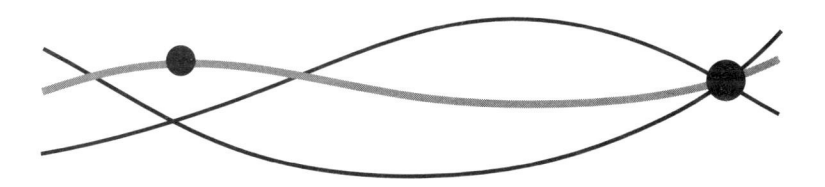

*Read Daniel 10:1–21*

In chapter 10 Daniel met Michael the angel, and we are introduced to the spiritual dimension involved in world government. This is an aspect to world history we do not see or hear much about, but it is very real.

Daniel placed the revelation of this chapter in the third year of Cyrus king of Persia. According to Ezra 1:1, the Lord moved the heart of Cyrus to allow the children of Israel to return to their homeland. In chapter 9 we saw how Daniel had realized this through the prophecy of Jeremiah and had prayed to this end. Several years had passed, and some of the Jewish exiles had returned to Jerusalem and were in the process of rebuilding the city and temple. Not everyone returned to Jerusalem. It appears from the context that Daniel remained in exile. If we understand that Daniel was an adolescent when he was captured, that he had spent seventy years in exile, and that this chapter opens in the third year of Cyrus, this would place Daniel well into his eighties at this point in time.

Notice in verse 2 that at the time of this vision, Daniel had been mourning for three weeks. We are not told why Daniel had been mourning, but during these three weeks Daniel fasted and did not anoint himself with lotion. In reality, he was doing without the luxuries of life because he had a deep burden on his heart. In Jerusalem at this time, the people of God were meeting with opposition from their neighbors who were trying to hinder the rebuilding of the city (see Ezra 4:1–5). It could be that Daniel had received news of this and was praying and fasting for a breakthrough in the lives of his people in Jerusalem.

It was on the twenty-fourth day of the first month that Daniel was standing on the bank of the Tigris River in Babylon. As he looked up, he saw a man dressed in linen with a fine gold belt around his waist, marking him as a person of dignity. Daniel noticed that his body was clear like chrysolite. In others words, his body resembled a transparent green jewel. Daniel compared his face to lightning. His eyes were like flaming torches, and his legs and arms were as shining as polished bronze. When he spoke it was as loud as a multitude of voices combined into one. Obviously, this figure standing before him was awesome and majestic. There were other people with Daniel when he saw this vision, but Daniel was the only one to see this man. The people with him, however, knew that something astounding was happening in their midst, and they were terrified. Commentators differ regarding the possible identity of this heavenly being—whether he was Christ or an angel.

The people with Daniel were so terrified that they ran away and hid, leaving Daniel by himself (verse 8). For Daniel the sight of this man in the vision was so overwhelming that his face turned deathly pale. He was left helpless (possibly unable to move or respond).

This man spoke to Daniel, and Daniel fell into a deep sleep with his face to the ground (verse 9). This would not have been a natural sleep. Did Daniel faint? Was he physically unconscious but still seeing the vision? It is not natural to sleep with one's face to the ground. The face to the ground is a posture of respect.

We are not told how long Daniel lay on the ground, but, eventually, he felt a hand touch him and lift him up. His body trembled as he remained on his knees. A voice spoke to him: "Daniel, you who are highly esteemed, consider carefully the words I am about to speak to you and stand up for I have now been sent to you" (verse 11). It must have been encouraging to Daniel to hear from this messenger that he was highly esteemed in the heavenly realms. Daniel was very precious to the Lord.

As Daniel stood trembling, the man told him not to be afraid. He told Daniel that from the first day that he set his mind to gain understanding and to humble himself before the Lord, God had heard his prayers. The man told Daniel that he had come in response to those prayers (verse 12).

What is particularly interesting here is that the heavenly being told Daniel that he had been held back or resisted for twenty-one days by the prince of the Persian kingdom (verse 13). We are led to believe that he would have come to Daniel sooner, but the prince of Persia kept him back. This verse raises several important questions.

What is the identity of the prince of Persia? This prince had resisted the heavenly being that stood before Daniel. It would appear from this that the prince of Persia was some sort of demonic spirit who had responsibilities in the region of Persia to carry out Satan's desires. It was this demonic spirit that resisted the angel or heavenly being that had come to Daniel in response to his prayer.

It is important that we understand what was happening here. There is a battle in the spiritual realm. The angels of God are at war with the demonic forces of hell. The angel who had come to Daniel had been doing battle with the demonic prince of Persia. The holy angel had been restrained for twenty-one days. We are not told why the angel of God was not able to conquer this prince sooner. The angel would have been detained even longer had it not been for Michael, one of the chief angels of God, who came to his aid. Together they were able to resist the demonic prince of Persia, and the first angel was able to

**Michael and the Persians** ● 65

continue his mission of explaining to Daniel the details of the vision he had seen.

This passage gives us a glimpse of the spiritual battle that rages in the heavenly realm. This battle is unseen to our human eye, but it is very real. The powerful human leaders of Persia were not the real enemies. They were being influenced by this demonic prince over Persia. Victory in the earthly realm could only come when the battle was won in the spiritual realm. The real battle was a spiritual battle.

We are reminded here that God allows the demonic forces a certain measure of rebellion and obstruction against his will, just as God allows humans a certain measure of free will against his commands. However, God is in control and overrides the limited power of demons and humans whenever his chooses to do so. Ultimately, God accomplishes all his purposes (Isaiah 46:10–11; Job 42:2).

As Daniel prayed, the battle in the heavens raged on. Unknown and unseen to the naked eye, a great war was taking place. We should not underestimate what happens when we pray. As we pray the spiritual forces of evil are being bombarded in the spiritual world.

As Daniel listened to what the angel was saying, he bowed his head toward the ground and was speechless (verse 15). As he stood there, someone who looked like a man touched his lips. Daniel opened his eyes and began to speak. Daniel told the angel how he was overcome with anguish because of the vision he had just seen. He felt helpless. The vision left Daniel physically and emotionally exhausted. In verse 17 Daniel did not even know how he could speak to the angel standing before him. His strength was gone, and he could hardly breathe. Such was the intensity of the vision Daniel saw that day.

The angel touched Daniel and said, "Do not be afraid, O man highly esteemed. Peace! Be strong now; be strong" (verse 19). Even as the angel spoke these words, Daniel could feel his body being filled with strength. The angel told Daniel that he would soon have to return to his battle with the prince of Persia.

When he had finished with the prince of Persia, the prince of Greece would take his place. He told Daniel that only he and Michael the angel were battling with these particular demonic forces. For the time being, however, he had come to Daniel to tell him the things that were to come to pass.

I find it amazing that this angel would be sent to Daniel in response to his prayer when there was such a terrible battle taking place. Obviously, Daniel was a vital part of the plan of God for victory over these demonic forces. The descriptive words "your prince" reveal that the angel Michael was sent by God to carry out divine purposes for Daniel and perhaps the whole Jewish nation at this time.

This chapter gives us a picture of the things that happen in the spiritual realm. It shows us how in this realm there is an intense battle taking place. It shows us that the angels of heaven are a vital part of that battle. These matters are extremely complicated, and we are only given glimpses of this reality. Daniel shared with us his brief view into this unseen sphere. What we need to understand is that the results of the battle in the spiritual realm will be evident on earth. We can be sure that there are angels fighting around us and protecting us as well. The holy angels constantly attend to the purposes of God in heaven and on earth. How encouraged we ought to be, because we know this.

*For Consideration:*

- What does this chapter teach us about the spiritual battle that rages in the spiritual realm?

- How does knowing something of the nature of this battle affect how we live as believers?

- What does this chapter teach us about the futility of our own human strength to fight a spiritual battle?

- What is the importance of prayer in the spiritual battle around us?

*For Prayer:*

- Thank God for the ministry of his angels on our behalf.
- Thank the Lord that he will win the battle.
- Ask the Lord to show you in a deeper way the nature of the battle that is around you.
- Ask the Lord to help you to see the role he wants you to play in the battle for souls.

# 11

# The Angel's Revelation: From Darius to Seleucus IV

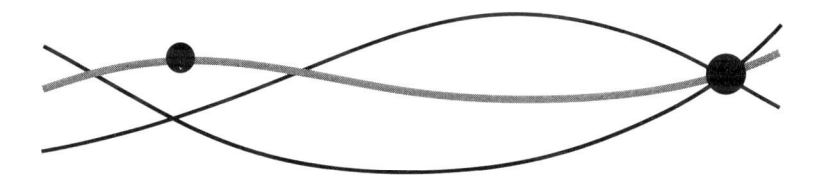

*Read Daniel 11:1–20*

The angel who was sent to Daniel told him in the last chapter that he had come to reveal the things that would happen in the coming years. What is amazing here is that while the angel was being resisted by demonic forces in the region, he knew all the details of how the battle was going to unfold. He knew that the Lord would win the battle, and he also knew that the unfolding of that wonderful plan would not be without difficulty.

The angel continued by telling Daniel how he had taken his stand to support and protect Darius the Mede in the first year of his reign. It is interesting to note here that though Darius was not a believer, the angel of the Lord was given charge to protect and strengthen him anyway. Darius, as an unbeliever, was an instrument in the hands of the Lord to accomplish his purpose on the earth of allowing the people of Judah to return to the Promised Land after their exile in Babylon.

In verse 2 the angel told Daniel that there would be three Persian kings and then a fourth who would be richer and more powerful than the others. When the fourth Persian king had gained power and wealth, he would stir up his people against the nation of Greece. Commentators identify this fourth Persian king as Xerxes (486–465 BC) who unsuccessfully attacked Greece. Persia would never be the same after this defeat.

In verse 3 the angel explained to Daniel that after this fourth king, another mighty king would appear who would rule with great power and do as he pleased. This king is identified with Alexander the Great of Greece who brought Greece to the forefront as a world power after conquering Persia. In chapter 8 Alexander the Great was pictured as a goat that attacked the Persian ram and trampled it underfoot.

Daniel was told in verse 4 that after this powerful leader (Alexander the Great) appeared, his empire would be broken up and parceled out to the four winds of heaven. It would not go to his descendants. The empire he left would not have the power it had under his control and would be uprooted and given to others.

Historically, after the death of Alexander the Great, this is exactly what happened to his empire. Alexander's son was murdered and his kingdom divided into four parts. Seleucus ruled the areas of Syria and Palestine. Cassander was given the regions of Macedonia, Thessaly, and Greece. Ptolemy ruled in Egypt, and Lysimachus ruled in Thrace and Asia Minor.

In verses 5–20 the angel focused on two of these kings whom he called "the king of the South" and "the king of the North." These directions are in relation to Israel. The southern kingdom refers to Egypt where the descendants of Ptolemy ruled, and the northern kingdom refers to Syria where the descendants of Seleucus ruled. The Promised Land stood between these two great powers, and it became territory that each kingdom battled over.

One of Ptolemy's satraps was a man by the name of Seleucus Nicator who would eventually become the king of the North in the region of Babylon, Media, and Syria. His power would even surpass that of Ptolemy, under whom he had served.

The angel told Daniel that after a certain number of years, there would be an alliance between the king of the South (Ptolemy) and one of his former commanders (Seleucus Nicator). This alliance would be the result of a marriage. The daughter would not retain her power, and the power of her husband would also be lost. This daughter would be "handed over" with all who supported her (verse 6).

Historians tell us that Ptolemy II of Egypt was having trouble with the king of the North, who at that time was Antiochus Theos, a descendant of Seleucus Nicator. To stop this trouble, he attempted to form an alliance by giving his daughter Berenice to Antiochus Theos who agreed to this marriage and divorced his wife, Laodice, to marry Berenice. This marriage sealed an agreement between the North and the South for a time.

Laodice, the divorced wife of Antiochus Theos, did not take well to being cast aside for Berenice and this political alliance. Being an influential woman, Laodice gained the support of a number of individuals and organized a campaign against Berenice. Antiochus Theos was poisoned and died. As for Berenice and her son, Laodice had them put to death and raised her own son Seleucus II to take the throne.

In verse 7 the angel told Daniel that one from the family line of this daughter of the North would attack the palace and be victorious over it. Historically, Ptolemy III (Euergetes), brother of Berenice, later avenged the death of his sister by attacking Syria. Daniel was told in verse 8 that this king would seize the gods, metal images, and other precious objects.

In verse 9 the angel explained to Daniel that the king of the North (Syria) would attack the king of the South (Egypt) but would have to retreat to his own country. His sons, however, would prepare for war and assemble a massive army that would sweep across the land like a flood. The battle would come as far as the "fortress." Historically, Seleucus II did attack territory held by Egypt and regained a certain measure of control. His son Antiochus III (Callinicus) would also wage war against

Ptolemy IV of Egypt but would be defeated even though he had a much bigger army (verse 11).

After defeating Antiochus III, Ptolemy IV would continue on his rampage and slay many thousands of people. The angel told Daniel that he would not remain triumphant (verse 12). Egypt's defeat would come.

In verse 13 Daniel was told that the king of the North (Antiochus III) would gather a large army, larger than the one he had gathered to defend himself in verse 10. The angel told Daniel that in those days many other nations would rise up against the king of Egypt. Violent men among Daniel's own people would also rebel against Egypt and join the forces of Antiochus III (verse 14). The Jews did support Antiochus III by providing him with supplies, but this attack did not accomplish what the Jews had hoped.

Egypt would retreat from a campaign against the North to the region of Phoenicia. Antiochus III built a siege ramp and defeated Egypt in this area about 200 BC. Egypt was powerless to resist him and was forced to surrender (verse 15).

Having conquered Egypt, Antiochus III would do as he pleased (verse 16). For a time there would be no one to resist him and his military efforts. He would even establish himself in the "Beautiful Land." This reference to the "Beautiful Land" may be a reference to the land of Judah. Antiochus III did establish his rule over the land of Judah. It is said that because the Jews helped him, by supplying him with provisions in his attempt to overthrow the king of Egypt, he favored them.

In an attempt to secure his kingdom and form an alliance with Egypt, ending the war between them, Antiochus III determined that he was going to give his daughter (Cleopatra) to Ptolemy V of Egypt. His hope was that Cleopatra would control Ptolemy V, a young boy of around ten years of age, for her father's benefit. As it turned out, however, Cleopatra loved her husband, Ptolemy V, more than she loved her father, and the plans of Antiochus III failed (see verse 17).

Because his plans for Egypt had failed, Antiochus III

would turn his attention to the Mediterranean coastlands, but this brought him into conflict with Rome. The angel told Daniel in verse 18 that Antiochus III would become very proud. That pride would be broken by a Roman general by the name of Lucius Cornelius Scipio Asiaticus who defeated Antiochus III in 190 BC (see verse 18). Antiochus III would return to his own country, but verse 19 tells us that he would stumble and be no more.

After Antiochus III was defeated by the Roman general, Rome imposed a tribute on him. This was part of the humbling of Antiochus III. Much of his riches were taken away. We are told that Antiochus III had to resort to pillaging to pay his debt. He was killed by a mob in an attempt to plunder a pagan temple in Elymais. Verse 19 states that he would "be seen no more."

When Seleucus IV succeeded Antiochus III, he heavily taxed his people to pay Rome and to maintain the splendor of his kingdom. This was an attempt to build up the wealth of the kingdom again and restore its glory. We are told that Seleucus IV would attempt to plunder the temple of Jerusalem for the glory of his kingdom. His Jewish tax collector, Heliodorus, poisoned him. Verse 20 states that he did not die in battle. This assassination set the stage for the Syrian persecution of the Jews that followed.

In this first section of chapter 11, the angel told Daniel in great detail how the events of the next several hundred years would unfold. These events occurred exactly as the angel said. We have details here regarding Persia, Greece, Syria, and Egypt. The events were predicted many years before they came to pass. The details are very precise.

This reminds us that this world is not in the hands of the enemy. God controls all the details of history. There are no surprises for God. While the path may seem long and hard, there is a divine plan. God is working out the details of history to accomplish his perfect will. His angels are doing battle against the forces of evil. If the Lord knows the details of the nations, he also knows all the details of your life and mine. All things will work out for the glory of God and the good of his people. This chapter ought to reassure us of this fact.

*For Consideration:*

- What do the prophetic details of this section reveal about God's knowledge and control of all that happens?

- What is the connection here between God's plan for history and the battle by which that plan will unfold? Does God's control of history mean that the spiritual war is over?

- What comfort and encouragement do you receive from this chapter in regard to your own personal life?

*For Prayer:*

- Thank the Lord that he is an all-knowing God and that there are no surprises for him.

- Thank the Lord that he knows all the details of your life as well.

- Thank him that victory is assured for his people.

# 12

# The Angel's Revelation: Antiochus IV Epiphanes

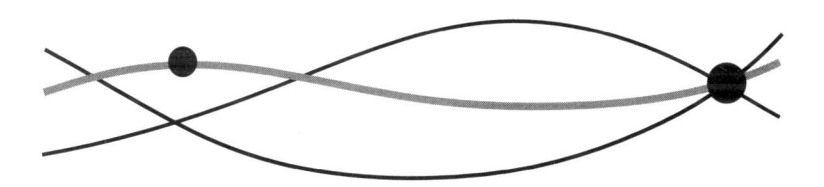

*Read Daniel 11:21–45*

As we continue to unfold the complex details of Daniel 11, we see how world history came to pass exactly as the angel told Daniel. Seleucus IV would be succeeded, as verse 21 says, by a very contemptible person who was not given the honor of royalty. Instead, he would invade the kingdom and seize it by trickery and deceit. Historically, Antiochus IV Epiphanes (175–164 BC) would take the throne of Syria after Seleucus IV. He was not the rightful heir to the throne, but, because the son of Seleucus IV was held hostage in Rome, the throne was seized by Antiochus Epiphanes. Antiochus Epiphanes corresponds to the little horn of chapter 8 (8:9–12, 23–25). Much attention is given to him in the text because he had such a devastating effect on Israel.

We understand that Antiochus Epiphanes would often lure his victims by offering them some sort of alliance and friendship and then break that alliance. Verse 22 tells us that a great army would be swept away before him, and a prince of the covenant would be destroyed. We know that he was successful against the great army of Egypt and that he had a Jewish high priest killed.

Verses 23–27 tell of different plots of Antiochus Epiphanes of Syria against Ptolemy VI of Egypt. He would conquer, loot, and divide his wealth among leaders to encourage their cooperation with his plans (verse 24). Egypt would try to defend itself against his attack but would not succeed. In verse 26 the angel told Daniel that those who ate the king's provisions would destroy him. This seems to refer to Ptolemy. His own counselors betrayed him and advised him to attack Syria. This led to his defeat. Antiochus Epiphanes was successful in part because he often pretended to be in alliance with Ptolemy to gain the advantage in the confusion.

After this defeat the two kings, Antiochus Epiphanes and Ptolemy VI, would sit at the table to discuss their future (verse 27). The hearts of both of these kings would be bent on evil and deception. They hated each other and their deliberations would be filled with lies and deceit. Nothing good would come from these discussions.

The angel told Daniel in verse 28 that the king of the North (Antiochus Epiphanes) would return to his country with great wealth. At that time his heart would be set against the holy covenant. This seems to be a reference to the people of God. He would take action against the Jews before returning to Syria in the north.

In 168 BC Antiochus Epiphanes participated in a Jewish revolt against the high priesthood in Jerusalem and took vengeance on those who opposed the blasphemy. He killed 80,000 people, took 40,000 prisoners, and sold another 40,000 as slaves. He entered the temple in Jerusalem and sacrificed pigs on the altar to desecrate it. He boiled the pigs' flesh and sprinkled the broth throughout the temple. Before he left Jerusalem, he took the gold and silver vessels from the temple with him. This was a horrific act of violent blasphemy against God and the Jewish nation.

In verse 29 the angel told Daniel that Antiochus Epiphanes

would again invade the South, but the outcome would be very different from the first time. He would be opposed by ships from the western coastlands, and he would lose heart (verse 30). Egypt, suspecting that Antiochus Epiphanes would return, hired Greek mercenaries. A Roman fleet in the area also sided with Egypt. Antiochus Epiphanes was forced to retreat and chose to vent his anger and frustration on the people of Jerusalem again.

In verse 30 the angel prophesied that he would choose to show favor on those who forsook the holy covenant. When Antiochus Epiphanes arrived in Jerusalem, he discovered that the worship of God had been reestablished after he had desecrated the temple. This infuriated him. He had the temple pillaged, killed the worshipers, and abolished sacrifices (verse 31). Antiochus Epiphanes tried to rid the Promised Land of Judaism. He attacked Jerusalem on the Sabbath and burned the city. He forbade Jews, on pain of death, to practice the Mosaic law and commanded them to conform to the Greek religion. The temple in Jerusalem was consecrated to Zeus. In the place of the altar used for burnt offerings, Antiochus Epiphanes erected an idol of the Greek god Zeus. Antiochus Epiphanes identified himself with Zeus and ordered the Jews to worship him. This was a great abomination in the eyes of both the Jews and God. This act was referred to as the "abomination that causes desolation" (verse 31). Some commentators believe that both Daniel and Jesus prophesied that this act was only a preview of a similar abomination by another oppressor of God's people—the Antichrist (9:27; Matthew 24:15).

These days would be terrible days for the Jewish people. There would be some apostate Jews who would fall to the flattery and corruption of Antiochus Epiphanes. The angel told Daniel, however, that those who truly knew God would firmly resist this enemy (verse 32). They would not give in to his evil nor turn their backs on their God. For their persistence, many would suffer. Some would be killed by the sword; some would be burned to death; and some would be captured and plundered (verse 33).

In this time of tremendous persecution and opposition, Judas Maccabeus, a Jew, would rise up to defend his people against the persecution of Antiochus Epiphanes. The Maccabeans were quite severe with those who had turned their backs on the Jewish faith. They were successful in raising an army to combat Antiochus Epiphanes. Verse 34 tells us that the Jews would receive a little help. This help came in the form of the Maccabeans. Even those Jews who were not sincere in their faith found strength in Judas Maccabeus and joined him in the revolt. While these weaker brothers had very likely conformed to the decree of Antiochus Epiphanes and worshiped the idol of Zeus, they saw the popular support that the Maccabeans were receiving and became willing to take a stand against the foreign oppressor. They joined the resistance against Antiochus Epiphanes.

The extent of the persecution was such that even the wise would stumble under the cruel arm of Antiochus Epiphanes (verse 35). God allowed this for a time so that his people would be purified. At the appointed time all persecution would stop. The strongest among them would be tested because God was purifying them. What is important for us to understand here is that at the appointed time God would step in and break this evil.

In the meantime, this evil king would continue to do as he pleased (verse 36). He would exalt and magnify himself above every god and would even say horrible things against the God of gods (the God of Israel). The blasphemy of Antiochus Epiphanes would be great, but he would only be successful until his time came to an end. God knew the day and hour when he would be broken. This matter was under God's control.

Antiochus Epiphanes would not honor the gods of his fathers. He would not honor the gods the women of his day sought after nor would he worship any other god. Instead, he would exalt himself above them all and lift himself up as a god, requiring that people bow down and worship him (verse 37). His god was brute strength and force (verse 38). He wanted to control everything he saw, and used all his treasures to become more dominant. Power was his idol, and this was what he lived and fought for.

Antiochus Epiphanes would greatly honor those who acknowledged him by offering them positions of power and prestige (verse 39). He would divide up the land he had conquered and use it to reward those who gave him what he wanted.

Verses 40–45 are difficult to understand. Most commentators agree that they do not fit the history of Antiochus Epiphanes. This has led many to understand that the conclusion of this chapter refers to the final days. Antiochus Epiphanes, as a terrible enemy of the people of God, is seen as a symbol of the Antichrist who is to come in the end times.

In verse 40 the angel told Daniel that in the time of the end, the king of the South and the king of the North would storm out against a great enemy of God's people with chariots, cavalry, and a great fleet of ships. Despite this opposition the enemy of God's people would continue his evil campaign. He would invade Jerusalem (the Beautiful Land), and many other countries would fall under his control. However, Edom, Moab, and Ammon (present-day Jordan) would be delivered from his hands. He would gain control over great wealth, taking the riches of the Egyptians, Libyans, and Nubians.

In the height of his power, however, the angel told Daniel in verse 44 that reports from the east and the north would alarm him. He would set out in even greater fury to destroy and annihilate many more. He would ultimately pitch his tent in the region of Jerusalem, but his end would come, and no one would help him on the day of his defeat. As we have said, it is difficult to reconcile these last events with the reign of Antiochus Epiphanes. These events, therefore, may look forward to another time in history. Many commentators see here a reference to the time of the Antichrist that John spoke of in the end times. If this is the case, the particular details of this passage will be unfolded in a future time.

Daniel realized that the coming days would be very difficult for the Jewish people. Tremendous persecution would break out against them. Many would die. It is hard to understand why the Lord allows such evil men like Antiochus Epiphanes to live. What is clear, however, is that the Lord knew every detail of what was going to happen. The amount of detail here is astounding. Long before these things happened, they were told to Daniel for him to record.

Nothing takes God by surprise. While we do not understand all the details of these events and why the Lord allows them, we do know that God will triumph in the end. In this, at least, we can take great courage.

*For Consideration:*

- What comfort do you find in the fact that the details of these events were predicted many years before they actually happened?

- Would you be able to face the persecution that the angel told Daniel would take place in the land of Jerusalem?

- What do we learn here about the terrible evil of the real enemy, Satan, and how he uses leaders to accomplish his evil plans?

*For Prayer:*

- Thank the Lord that we see here that good will triumph over evil in the end.

- Ask the Lord to help you to be faithful in what he has called you to do right now.

- Thank him that he has kept you in your difficulties.

- Ask the Lord to bless and strengthen those who have to suffer for their faith today.

# 13

# The Final Victory

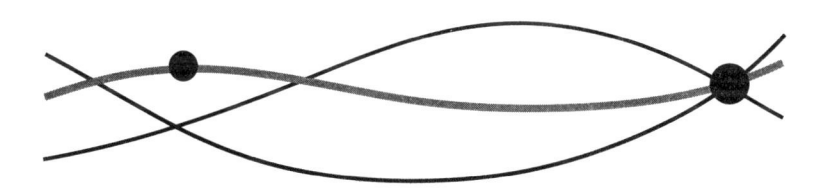

*Read Daniel 12:1–13*

Daniel's vision came to a conclusion in chapter 12. Here we see that the Lord will overcome and conquer the enemies of his people. This chapter emphasizes the faithfulness of God to his promises to Israel.

In verse 1 the angel continued to speak to Daniel and told him that in the final days, Michael would arise. It is important that we note what this verse tells us about Michael. Michael is a great prince who protects the people of God. Michael is one of the chief angels of God in heaven. He is described as an archangel in Jude 1:9. He is seen doing battle with the great dragon in Revelation 12:7. Here we see that one of his responsibilities is to protect and keep the people of God. What a comfort it is for us to know that the angels of heaven are given charge over our welfare.

It is important to note here that while Michael was given charge over the people of God, this did not mean that they would never have any difficulty or struggle in life. We have seen already in this book of Daniel that there is an intense struggle in the spiritual realm. We have seen the suffering that the Jews endured under Antiochus Epiphanes. In verse 1 we are told that in the end times, there would be a time of distress that had not happened since the beginning of nations.

What we need to see here in verse 1 is that while the battle would be very fierce, everyone whose name was "written in the book" would be delivered. We are not told about this book, but it is some kind of divine written record for God's purposes. God would protect his people and keep them during this difficulty. As the days of the end approach, we can expect that there will be increasing struggle, but we can take comfort in the fact that God is able to care for his own.

In verse 2 the angel told Daniel that the day would come when those who had been asleep would awake. There would be a resurrection from the dead. Many would lose their lives for the Lord, but for these individuals there was a wonderful hope of resurrection. Those who had been faithful would go on to everlasting life. For those who had rejected the Lord, however, things would be radically different. They would be raised to everlasting contempt and judgment. This clearly is the teaching of the New Testament (Matthew 25:46; John 5:28–29).

Daniel was told that those who were wise would shine like the brightness of the heavens and would lead many to righteousness (verse 3). There was a wonderful hope for those who were wise. To be wise in this context means to know God and be faithful to him despite the terrible things that would happen on the earth. A time of persecution would not be a time to stop sharing the love of God. On the contrary, this would be a time to be even bolder in faith.

Daniel was told that he was to seal up the words of this prophecy until the days of the end. The matters relating to the final judgment and the resurrection of the dead were not for the immediate future. These matters were for a distant future. It was not necessary for the people of God to understand all the details of this matter for the moment. The time would come when these words would make sense.

The day was coming, the angel told Daniel, when knowledge would increase on the earth and people would have a deep hunger for it (verse 4). They would move here and there in search of knowledge. It appears that there is a connection between the sealed words of the scroll that Daniel wrote and the knowledge the angel spoke of here. This has lead some to assume that the angel was speaking of a time when there would be a hunger to understand the truth that Daniel was speaking about here in this passage.

As Daniel spoke to the angel, he looked and there before him stood two other angels, one on each side of a river. One of these angels spoke to a man clothed in linen above the waters of the river and asked him how long it would be before these things were accomplished (verse 6). The angel inquired about the duration of Israel's final persecution and deliverance.

In response, the man in linen lifted up his right hand toward heaven and swore by him who lives forever (God) that these events would take place in "a time, times and half a time" (verse 7). Commentators are generally agreed that the term *time* refers to a year, *times* refers to two years, and *half a time* refers to half a year. In other words, the man in linen said that the final persecution of God's people would take place in a period of three and a half years. Within that time the power of the holy people would be broken, but there would be a limit to their intense suffering. The enemy could not go beyond God's appointed time.

The number three and a half is often used in the Scriptures as a time of persecution and trial. We see, for example, in Revelation 11:1–2 that John told his readers that the temple would be trampled for forty-two months or three and a half years: "I was given a reed like a measuring rod and was told, 'Go and measure the temple of God and the altar, and count the worshipers there. But exclude the outer court; do not measure it, because it has been given to the Gentiles. They will trample on the holy city for 42 months.'"

In Revelation 11:3 we are told that two witnesses would

witness for 1,260 days or three and a half years: "And I will give power to my two witnesses, and they will prophesy for 1,260 days, clothed in sackcloth." In Revelation 13:5 the beast that was to come would be given power to exercise authority over the earth for forty-two months or three and a half years: "The beast was given a mouth to utter proud words and blasphemies and to exercise his authority for forty-two months."

The same thing was prophesied here in verse 7. The persecution of God's people would last for three and a half years and then be broken. The similarity of this passage and the passages we have quoted in Revelation has led many to believe that they refer to similar events. In the last days, there would be a great persecution of the godly that would last for a period of three and a half years. Not all believers will escape persecution. Some will be called to suffer greatly. God will limit it, however, and he will be victorious in the end.

Daniel was somewhat confused. He asked the angel for more details concerning the end of this persecution and what would happen (verse 8). Daniel was told to go his way. The details of this prophecy were sealed until the time of the end. Only then would the prophecy be understood by the people of God. God does not always burden us with details that are not necessary for us to understand. When the time is right, he will reveal to his people what is necessary.

The angel did tell Daniel in verse 10 that many would be purified, refined, and made spotless. Obviously, there was a purpose for this persecution of three and a half years. God would use this time to purify his people and bring many to salvation. Notice, however, that the wicked would continue in their wicked ways. The angel predicted that some people would resist God to the end. Unlike the wise righteous who would understand what was happening, the wicked would not be purified by this trial. The proud arrogance of the wicked would ultimately be their downfall. While the persecution of God's people would last for a period of three and a half years, the judgment of the wicked will last forever (Matthew 25:41, 46).

Daniel was reminded in verse 11 that from the time that the daily sacrifice was abolished and the abomination was set up, there would be 1,290 days or three and a half years plus 30 days. The angel told Daniel that the person who reached the end of 1,335 days would be blessed. Some would have to face this persecution longer than others. While they did have to endure longer than some, their blessing would also be greater. God would reward faithfulness. Commentators differ in their explanations of these extra days added to the original 1,260 of prophesied persecution. Some say these verses were meant to encourage believers to continue in faithfulness for the extended time, knowing that God is in control and will abundantly reward all faithfulness.

As for Daniel, the angel told him that he was to go his way until the end (verse 13). He would rest or die, and when the time was right, he would rise up to receive his reward.

While the details of this prophecy can be somewhat confusing, we understand that severe persecution was prophesied for the people of God. These trials, though very difficult, would not last forever. The enemy was only given a certain time to persecute the people of God and then would be cut off. Michael the angel was given charge over God's people. Those who persevered to the end would be raised to eternal life. Those who rejected the Lord would be raised to face eternal judgment.

There is a real battle before us. This battle will intensify as the days of the end approach. May God give us strength to resist evil and do good, always looking to the Lord to supply what is needed for us to be faithful to our gracious Savior, who is our shield and our great reward.

*For Consideration:*

- What does this passage teach us about the nature of the battle that is raging around us?

- What does this passage teach us about the difficulties that we must sometimes face in this life?

- Would you be able to resist the enemy in these times of persecution?

- What comfort do you find in the fact that the Lord limits the persecution his people have to endure?

*For Prayer:*

- Ask the Lord to give you the grace to persevere to the end.

- Thank him that he has placed his angels over us to keep us in these difficult times.

- Thank him that while the enemy may sometimes rage around us, his time of evil is limited.

# Hosea

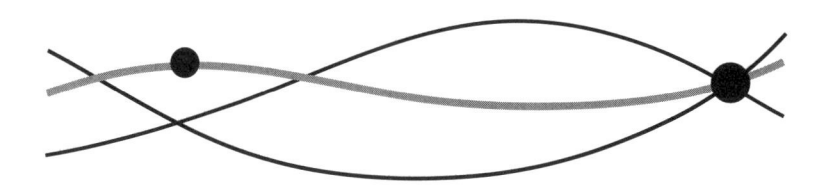

# 14

# Introducing the Prophet

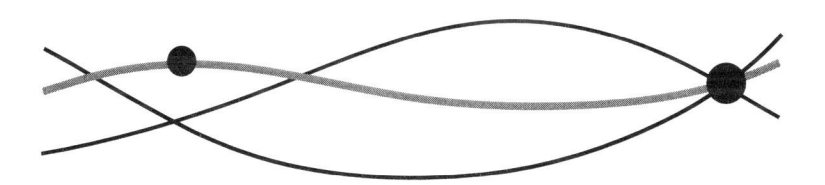

*Read Hosea 1:1–11*

Let me introduce you to the prophet Hosea. He had a lengthy ministry from about 755–710 BC during the reigns of Uzziah, Jotham, Ahaz, and Hezekiah, which were all kings of the southern kingdom of Judah, and during the reign of Jeroboam who was king of the northern kingdom of Israel. When Hosea began his ministry under Uzziah, God's people in Judah were living in prosperity and ease. Hosea watched, however, as Uzziah turned his heart away from God. He agonized as Ahaz led Judah into idolatry. He witnessed the spread of Baal worship throughout the land. He stood by helplessly as the doors of the temple were barred shut. He was stunned at the news that Ahaz had sacrificed his son on the altar to his pagan gods. When Hezekiah came to the throne, Hosea breathed a sigh of relief. What joy it must have brought to his heart to see repairs being made to the temple he loved so dearly. Never very far from his mind, however, was the prophecy of Isaiah, his contemporary who predicted the coming of Babylon to take away the wealth of Judah. Concerning the northern kingdom of Israel, he watched Jeroboam lead his people for forty-one years into the evil practices of the surrounding pagan nations.

Hosea prophesied at a time when there was a general turning away from the Lord in both kingdoms. Those kings who began their reigns by serving God fell quickly into pride. Particularly under the reign of Ahaz, the nation of Judah reached its lowest point. With the temple doors closed, the worship of Baal flourished. In the nation of Israel, God seemed to be the farthest thing from the minds of the people. Yet the major theme of Hosea is God's loyal love for his people in spite of their defiant sin and his necessary judgment.

Names in the Bible are very important. A name often represents the character or ministry of the individual. Hosea's name means "salvation" or "deliverance." His calling was to proclaim a message of salvation and deliverance to God's people. Though they had fallen deeply into sin, Hosea was to reach out to them and offer them deliverance and salvation from the Lord.

The reputation of Hosea's wife left much to be desired. She was unfaithful to her husband and was a prostitute. Verse 2 leads us to believe that she had several children out of wedlock. God asked Hosea to adopt these children as his own.

Their marriage was symbolic of the relationship between God and his people. God had entered into a covenant agreement with his people, but, like Hosea's wife, they were unfaithful to him. Hosea would experience in his marriage what God experienced with Israel and Judah. His messages would be filled with passion because of his experience with his own wife's adultery. The people to whom Hosea preached would see their unfaithfulness to God mirrored in the prophet's marriage. Hosea not only spoke a prophetic message to his people but he also lived a prophetic lifestyle mirroring what he spoke from God.

Hosea's wife was Gomer. The word *Gomer* means "complete" or "to come to an end." We cannot miss the significance of her name. The time of the end was coming for God's people.

God would not hesitate to deal with them according to their sins. There is a real contrast here in these names. Gomer represented the completeness of sin and the inevitable judgment that awaited the people of God. Hosea represented the deliverance and salvation that could be theirs if they repented and turned to God. We will see more of this symbolism in their marriage at a later point.

Hosea and Gomer had three children. Their first son was Jezreel, which means "God will scatter" (verse 5). Hosea was to call his son Jezreel as a prediction of God's judgment. Jezreel was also the name of an Israelite town where Jehu of Israel massacred the entire family of King Ahab and many others (2 Kings 9–10). God would punish the household of Jehu for going beyond the Lord's command. The name Jezreel not only looked back to this massacre, however, it also looked forward in time to another massacre that would take place in the Valley of Jezreel. Here Israel's bow, a symbol of military force, would be broken by the conquering nation of Assyria in 722 BC. The name Jezreel was used as a prophecy to the people of Israel of a coming day of judgment.

Their second child was a girl named Lo-Ruhamah. Her name means "not loved" or "no mercy." She reminded the people of Israel that the Lord would no longer show love and mercy to them. The time of judgment had come. They had every opportunity to repent of their sins, but they refused. Now it was too late. While there was still hope for Judah, Israel's fate was sealed. What a shock this was to the people of Israel who felt that the patience of God had no end.

Lo-Ammi was the third child born to this couple. His name literally means "not my people." God had ceased to see these rebellious Israelites as his people. They had broken their covenant relationship with him. These particular people were no longer his people, and he was no longer their God. Those who refused to repent were without hope and without God. Their judgment was sealed.

It is helpful to remember here that at this time the origi-

Introducing the Prophet ● 91

nal nation of Israel had divided into two different kingdoms. The northern kingdom went by different names, such as Israel, Samaria, and Ephraim. At this point in history, the northern kingdom was very far from the Lord, and he declared that he would bring an end to it (verses 4 and 6). The southern kingdom was called Judah and was less evil and had some good kings. Therefore, God did not declare an end to Judah (verse 7).

From verse 10 we understand that while there was no hope for these particular individuals of Hosea's day, God would not forget his covenant with Abraham. A time was coming when another generation would again be called the "sons of God." A faithful remnant from the kingdoms of Israel and Judah would be reunited under one leader. Some believe that this prophecy was fulfilled when faithful worshipers of God returned from the Babylonian exile as one nation (Judah) under the ministry of Ezra and Nehemiah to rebuild the city of Jerusalem. It may also look further ahead to a great work of God to bring Israel to salvation in Christ (Romans 9:25–29). Whereas Jezreel had symbolized a broken and massacred Israel, that broken nation would again rejoice in the goodness of God.

The moral and religious immorality of Hosea's day would cause God to judge the northern kingdom of Israel. Because of Israel's willful and persistent rebellion, she would perish without God and without hope. She would suffer the consequences of her actions. By God's grace, however, a faithful remnant of her descendants would be given another chance. Unlike Jehu, who wiped out the entire family of Ahab, God would not punish all the children for the sins of the fathers. While the fathers would perish without God, he would renew his covenant with their children.

God extends his gracious hand to us today. He freely offers us deliverance and salvation. This offer, however, is a limited-time offer. There is a day when God will cease his pleading and commence judgment. If you can hear his voice today, do not harden your heart. The day may come when you will no longer hear him call.

*For Consideration:*
- If you are married, what has your relationship with your spouse taught you about God?
- What impact do you think Gomer's lifestyle had on Hosea's ministry? How would their relationship be accepted in a modern church setting?
- What price did Hosea's children have to pay because of their father's ministry? Do children of pastors and missionaries today have a price to pay?
- What does this passage teach us about the grace and mercy of God?

*For Prayer:*
- Take a moment to pray for your pastor, his wife, and their children. Ask God to help them with the challenges they face.
- Ask God to help you to reflect his love for his people through your marriage and your lifestyle.
- Thank God for the commitment of Hosea to remain faithful to God despite the problems he had in his own marriage and life. Ask God to give you this type of commitment.
- Thank the Lord that he is a God of wonderful compassion and forgiveness.
- Take a moment to pray for a friend or loved one who has not yet accepted the Lord.

# 15

# The Discipline of a Loving Father

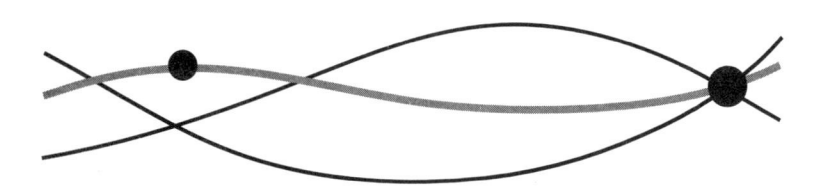

*Read Hosea 2:1–15*

One of the things that never ceases to amaze me is how a parent can be angry with a child and still reach out in love with a big hug. Any parent knows that love and discipline walk hand in hand. There are times in our lives when we experience the heavy hand of God's discipline. In these times we may wonder if God has forsaken us, because he seems far away. Like a rebellious child, Israel had wandered from God. Despite her sin, God still loved her. In love he would discipline her to draw her back to himself. And in that day, the Israelites would again be God's people and know that God's mercy had been shown (verse 1).

In verse 2 Israel is pictured as a wife and mother, and God is her husband. Because of her unfaithfulness, Israel had ceased to be God's wife. She had given herself to another. She broke her covenant vows and worshiped foreign gods. If Israel did not repent, her punishment would be severe. As a loving parent, God warned her of punishment so that she would have every opportunity to repent.

In verse 3 Hosea told Israel that if she did not repent, God would strip her naked and make her as barren as the desert. Over the years God had richly blessed Israel. She had been the envy of the nations. By her rebellion, however, she exchanged her blessing for a curse. She would lose everything and be exposed to the ridicule of other nations. Her beautiful land would be reduced to a parched wilderness that produced no crops and supported no livestock.

God reminded Israel in verses 4–5 that the children she had conceived in adultery did not belong to God. God would not love them and protect them as his own covenant children. We should understand here that these children were not innocent victims. God was not judging the children for the sins of their parent. They had chosen to follow the ways of their rebellious mother. Like her, they lusted after other gods. Many generations of Israelites had grown up in full and open rebellion against their covenant with God. They would be punished along with their parents for their individual sins. It is important to note here that children suffer many consequences for their parents' sins and their nations' sins, but God deals with each person on an individual basis.

God would not completely abandon the nation of Israel. Because of his grace, he would keep her from destroying herself. He told her through Hosea in verse 6 that he would block her path with thorn bushes. He would wall her in so that she could not find her way. Though she sought her lovers, she would never find them. Her lusts would never be satisfied outside of his true, covenant love.

Maybe you too have had your moments of rebellion and wandering from the Lord. In your wandering, however, you had no peace. Your lusts were never satisfied, and you had no contentment. Joy and satisfaction were far removed from you. Your soul was irritated as God's blessings were removed. You realized that you were getting nowhere and were being blocked. God in his grace was hedging you in and keeping you from completely destroying yourself.

**The Discipline of a Loving Father** ● 95

Israel would come to realize the blessings she had in her God. Broken, she would return to her husband. She would return because God had not forsaken her as a nation. She would return because God is full of mercy, grace, and forgiveness. She would return because God loved her too much to let her go.

God would work out all things for good, but Israel would lose much in the process. Because she had not recognized God as the source of her blessings, he would take away her grain, wine, and oil (verse 8). He would remove his blessing from her because he would not let anyone take her out of his hands. He would expose her before her lovers so that they would turn from her. As long as she had something to offer other nations, they were more than willing to remain in alliances with her. But when she became destitute, they dropped her like a dirty rag. Only when this happened would Israel turn her heart to God. The removal of her blessings was a blessing in itself. This would be the means through which she would be restored to her husband, but this process would be a lengthy and difficult one.

While Israel had turned her back on God, she continued to be involved in religious activities. She still practiced her yearly festivals and New Moon celebrations. She observed the Sabbath days and appointed feasts. In so doing, she blasphemed the name of the Lord because she mixed the worship of God with the worship of the false gods of the surrounding nations. The day was coming when she would no longer be free to practice the Mosaic law (verse 11). Assyria would invade and take her temple and her religious objects from her. Her land, with its deep religious significance, would be given to another. The vines and the fig trees (symbols of the rich blessings of the covenant with God) would be ruined. The land of promise would be overrun by thickets and wild animals. Israel had forsaken her covenant with God, and the day was coming when she would justly suffer the consequences of her rebellious acts (see 2 Kings 17:7–18; Deuteronomy 28). She had decked herself with jewelry and gone after the false god Baal, but she had forgotten the Lord (verse 13).

Hosea told his people in verse 14 that God would lure them into the desert. The desert is a barren place. It is a place of humiliation. When God had humbled his people and brought them to the point where they were finally willing to listen to him, he would speak tenderly to them. Hosea said that the Valley of Achor would become a door of hope. *Achor* means "trouble." It was in the Valley of Achor that God's people mourned their defeat at Ai because of Achan's sin (see Joshua 7). In this valley of trouble and mourning over sin, there would be a glimmer of hope. God would extend his gracious hand to his people in forgiveness and renewed blessing. There would again be victories for his children. In the Valley of Achor songs of deliverance would rise from the lips of his people like those they sang as they left the land of Egypt after their four hundred years of bondage. Israel would be restored. She would return to her husband (verse 16). These victories would only come, however, when Israel had come to the place of mourning for her sins. Here, by means of confession and forgiveness of sin, God's blessing would be restored.

Israel had abandoned her God. She had proven to be an unfaithful wife. Though she was unfaithful, God would be faithful to his covenant. He would punish her and humble her so that she would return to him. Despite her rebellion he would speak tenderly to her (verse 14). He would not allow anyone to take her from his hands (verse 10). In her trials she would come to the place of repentance and confession of sin. When she repented God would restore her to full communion with him.

This passage is an illustration of the grace of God. He extends unmerited favor to his people. Through the prophet Hosea, he reaches out to us as well. He calls all who have wandered dangerously away from the fold to return. Though we wander from him, he chases after us. He will not let us go. With arms open wide, he calls us to himself. Our rebellion has been great, but his grace is abundantly greater. Don't put him off another minute. Cast off all resistance and pride, and run to his open arms right now.

*For Consideration:*

- What do we learn here about the discipline of God in our lives? What is the purpose of that discipline?

- God's discipline is a proof of his love for us. Do you agree with this statement? Why?

- Can you think of a time when God hedged you in and kept you from wandering dangerously away from him? How did he bring you back or keep you from falling?

*For Prayer:*

- Thank the Lord for the times he has kept you from falling away from him and restored you to himself.

- Thank the Lord for his wonderful patience with us as his people. Thank him that his love for us does not diminish even when we fall into sin.

- Do you know a Christian who is wandering today? Ask God to keep this person from wandering too far. Ask him to do what it takes to bring this individual back to himself.

# 16

# Reconciliation

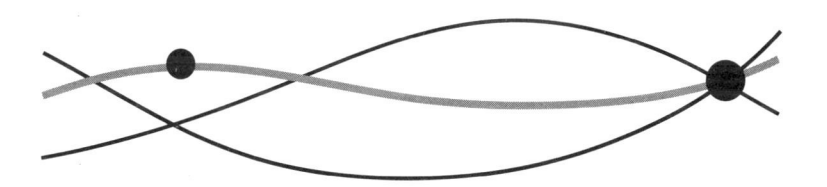

*Read Hosea 2:16–3:5*

How would you describe your relationship with God? For some, God is a distant master. Others see him as a loving friend. At this point in her history, Israel's relationship with God was on a master-servant level. Israel's sin had driven a wedge between her and her God. They related strictly on a business level. There was no intimacy.

The day was coming, however, when Israel would repent of her sins and return to God. On that day Israel would call God her husband. She would no longer call him master. There is a big difference between a master and a husband. The difference is principally one of relationship. God was telling his people that the time was coming when they would no longer see him as a harsh master but as a loving husband.

Some commentators note that because the word for master (*baali*) is the same word used to speak of the false gods of Baal worship, God was asking the people to refrain from calling him master so as not to confuse him with the Baals. Other commentators believe that the people of God were mixing the Mosaic law with Baal worship. God wanted nothing to do with this.

Hosea promised that the day was coming when the name of the Baals would be removed from the lips of his people (verse 17). Their hearts would be so devoted to God that they would not even desire to speak the name of Baal again. On that day God would pour out his blessings on them. He would make a covenant with the beasts of the field and the creatures of the earth. They would act favorably toward his people. Israel would live in safety without fear of war. The bow and the sword would be abolished (verse 18). God would enter an intimate and personal relationship with his people. Some commentators believe this was fulfilled by Christ's first coming. Others believe this has not been completely fulfilled and awaits Christ's millennial kingdom.

Notice what God said about this relationship through Hosea. First, this relationship would be binding for all time. "I will betroth you to me forever," God told his people in verse 19. Nothing would separate his people from him. Second, we see that this relationship would be "in righteousness and justice." The prophet Ezekiel prophesied in Ezekiel 36:26–27 that God would give his people a new heart: "I will give you a new heart and put a new spirit in you; I will remove from you your heart of stone and give you a heart of flesh. And I will put my Spirit in you and move you to follow my decrees and be careful to keep my laws."

The day was coming when all unfaithfulness and rebellion would cease. God's people would serve him with a pure heart. Their lives would be so changed that they would willingly conform to God's standard of righteousness and justice.

Third, this new relationship with Israel would be characterized by love. She would no longer serve God because she was required by law to do so. She would serve him out of a heart that truly loved him. God too would deal with her in compassion. Despite her shortcomings, God's grace would be showered on her.

Fourth, God's people had been accused of spiritual adultery. They had been responsible for breaking their covenant vows with God. This time, however, things would change. This new relationship with God would be built on faithfulness (verse 20). Their hearts would be consecrated to God. Nothing would distract them from serving the Lord.

Finally, their new relationship would be built on the acknowledgment of the Lord. What does it mean to acknowledge the Lord? It means that God's people would recognize him in all they did. They would accept their obligations toward him and live under his watchful eye. They would be conscious of his involvement in their everyday activities. Their hearts would bow in thankfulness and praise to God for his working in both the good and the bad of life.

Verses 21 and 22 tell us that Israel would again experience the blessing of God. God would speak to the skies and the earth and they would cause the ground to produce crops. Jezreel would again be blessed. The name Jezreel, meaning "God will scatter," can symbolize a blessing because the scattering can refer to seeds for crops.

The worship of the fertility god Baal was to assure the regular harvest of crops. The curse of God prevailing on the land proved to God's people that Baal was powerless. God showed his people that it was he who provided for their harvest and not Baal. Their blessing would return only when their relationship with him was restored.

In verses 22 and 23 God made some symbolic promises to the children of Hosea and Gomer. These prophetic promises, while given to Hosea's children, represented what God was going to do for Israel. Jezreel, the first child, who represented the judgment of God on the land, would again experience blessing. Lo-Ruhamah, Hosea's second child, whose name meant "not loved," would again know God's deep love. Lo-Ammi, "not my people," would again be called the people of God.

In his judgment God would not forsake mercy. He would not abandon his covenant. There was still a future for the covenant nation. He would reach out in love and compassion again to his people. To illustrate this future reconciliation between God and his people, the Lord asked Hosea to return to his wife (3:1). It appears that she had been seeing another man. Despite her unfaithfulness, Hosea was to take her back and love her as the Lord loved Israel. He wanted to shower her with his love and blessing. He wanted to forgive her for her adultery and the hurt she had caused him.

We discover that Hosea had to buy his wife back (3:2). We are not given the reason for this. What we need to understand, however, is that when Hosea had first taken Gomer as his wife, he paid a bridal price to her parents. She had now given herself to another. Though she was rightfully Hosea's, he bought her back. This is what the Lord did for us. Though we were in the wrong, he bought us back with his own life.

Because Hosea had bought her back, Gomer was no longer free to engage in her adulterous relationships. For a certain period of time, Gomer was not even permitted to have sexual relations with Hosea her husband. Throughout this time she was separated not only from her lovers but also from her true husband. During this period of deprivation, Gomer would have plenty of time for reflection.

This is what would happen to the people of God (3:4). They too would go through a period of deprivation. They would be deprived of political leadership, with no king or prince to lead them. They would be without sacrifice to offer the God of Israel or sacred stone to worship Baal (see 2 Kings 3:2). They would be without ephod and idol. The ephod was the garment worn by the priest in his service of God. God's people would be without priests to lead them in worship of the true God and without idols to worship the false gods. This is what would happen to God's people when they were forced into exile, and it may also refer to God's present dealings with the nation of Israel.

What would be the result of this period of deprivation? Israel would come trembling to God her husband. She would gain a new appreciation for him and his love for her. She would have time to reflect on her sin and unfaithfulness. Her trembling in the last days would be the result of her knowledge of personal guilt (see Revelation 1:7). When she returned to the Lord, she would be forgiven and again experience God's blessings in her life.

God wanted a close and intimate relationship with his people. Though they had turned their backs on him, he still wanted them as his own. He was willing to forgive them. There is hope for the wanderer in this passage. Through his prophet Hosea, the Lord calls out to us today. He calls us to cease all our wanderings and completely return to him. He has redeemed us through the blood of Christ, and he will restore us in love.

*For Consideration:*

- How would you describe your relationship with God? Is it a master-servant relationship or a husband-wife relationship?

- What does this passage tell us about the type of relationship God desires with his people? What does he expect of us in our relationship with him?

- What was God willing to do to redeem sinners?

- What holds you back from intimate fellowship with God?

*For Prayer:*

- Thank the Lord for his desire to enter into an intimate fellowship with you.

- Ask him to reveal to you those things which hold you back from experiencing this communion with him.

- Ask God to give you his heart for those who have hurt or offended you. Ask him to give you grace to forgive them.

# 17

# Sowing Seeds of Evil

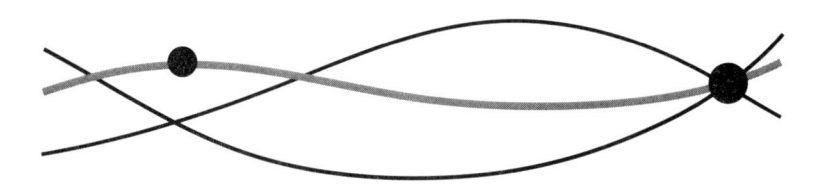

*Read Hosea 4:1–5*

While visiting us sometime ago, my in-laws noticed the beautiful lupines growing everywhere in the fields around us. They were attracted to these flowers and took home a package of seeds to plant in their yard. Lupines are one of those flowers that, once rooted, will quickly take over an entire field. Where I live this flower is considered to be a nuisance. A very similar thing was happening in Israel. God's people were planting seeds of evil. Very quickly they found themselves overwhelmed by the wickedness they had been sowing in their nation.

The people of Israel had broken their covenant vows with God. They had been unfaithful to him by pursuing false gods and immoral religious practices. Shrines to these foreign deities sprang up all over the land.

While some people may fall into the sin of unfaithfulness in a moment of weakness, the Israelites had gone beyond this. Not only had they been unfaithful to God, they were also guilty of no longer loving him. There was no love for God in the land (verse 1).

What could be worse than unfaithfulness and loss of love for a spouse? It would have to be a refusal to even acknowledge the years lived together in joy and happiness. This is what had happened to God's people. In the whole land, there was no acknowledgment of the Lord God. They had no desire to remember him. They had no desire to consult him. They did not even recognize that he was the source of their life. They had completely removed the God of Abraham, Isaac, and Jacob from their minds, hearts, and lives.

What was the result of the removal of God from the hearts and minds of the people? They were reaping what they had sowed. The land was filled with cursing. Because there was no love for God in their midst, love for each other diminished also, and the sinful nature was given free course. Truth and mercy disappeared, and the people began to curse each other and to curse God and his law (verse 2).

Dishonesty and violence flourished. To protect and prosper themselves, God's people resorted to lying, murder, stealing, and adultery. They were willing to kill in order to get what they wanted. Personal property, marriage, and life were no longer respected. God accused his people of breaking all bounds. All restrictions of social justice were thrown away. They were a people with no boundaries. They refused the self-discipline of righteousness and did as they pleased. Where love and forgiveness do not exist there is no end to sin.

God's people brought a great curse on their land (verse 3). The blessing of God was removed, and the land mourned and wasted away. This may refer to drought, which was a covenantal curse for disobedience (Deuteronomy 28:23 24). Every living thing suffered. The animals, birds, and fish were perishing. Sin brings havoc to all nature (see Romans 8:19–22).

God told his people through Hosea that they were not to bring charges against one another (verse 4). There was no one among them who could discern between good and evil. All of them were guilty. They were like people who brought charges against a priest if it served their purposes. They had no respect

Sowing Seeds of Evil ● 105

for righteousness. According to Deuteronomy 17:12, those who showed contempt for the servants of God deserved to die: "The man who shows contempt for the judge or for the priest who stands ministering there to the LORD your God must be put to death. You must purge the evil from Israel."

The Israelites stumbled day and night (verse 5). Their lives were made difficult by immorality at every level of society. They could no longer walk in peace and prosperity in the Lord. They stumbled like drunkards, ashamed and humiliated. Their false prophets stumbled with them. Their mother (symbol of the nation) was being destroyed.

Israel had sown the seeds of her own destruction. Wickedness quickly took over their land. Satan will never be happy with just a little corner of a life or a nation but will expand his dominion at every opportunity. Israel refused to acknowledge and love God and live in the preserving confines of his holy law. Instead she sowed seeds of unfaithfulness and reaped the covenantal curses that God had promised.

*For Consideration:*

- Why is it so important to deal with the sin in our lives?

- What hope is there for a nation that does not acknowledge God and sows seeds of unfaithfulness in the land?

- Why do we justify our sinful actions?

- What were the effects of Israel's sin on the earth and the economy of the land? Do you think your nation and its economy would be different if the people lived in obedience to the Lord God?

*For Prayer:*

- Does this section describe your nation? Take a moment to ask the Lord to deal with the sin in your nation before it completely takes over.

- Ask the Lord to reveal any sin in your life that needs to be confessed.

- Thank God for the wonderful blessing he pours out on those who love him.

# 18

# Accusations against the Priests

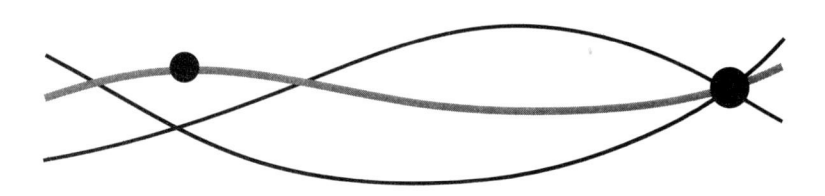

*Read Hosea 4:6–14*

The priests were the teachers of knowledge. They were responsible for instruction in the Word of God. Though they knew the Word of the Lord, the priests of Hosea's day rejected it (verse 6). They did not teach it to the people. The result was that the Israelites were physically and spiritually perishing through disobedience to God's law. They willfully lacked knowledge of God. Instead, they were filling their minds and lives with the pagan philosophies and religions of the nations around them. The Israelites were unprotected from sin and fell quickly into error and idolatry. God disowned them and their children as not being part of his covenant any longer. We need to remember that these people were not repentant sinners on whom God always has mercy, but God-haters and covenant-breakers who raised their children to be just like themselves.

As the number of priests increased, so did their sin (verse 7). They exchanged their "glory" for something disgraceful. The priest represented God's glory to the people. He was given the sacred charge of teaching and leading his people in the worship and service of the one true God. What a privilege this was. His ministry was one that should have been consumed with the beauty and wonder of God. There was no greater calling in Israel. But the power and splendor of this ministry was set aside for the shame of idolatry.

Beyond this, and even more important, was the fact that God was the true glory of the priest. The Lord himself ought to have been the priests' delight and glory. They turned their backs on him and chose rather to follow the pagan ways of the nations around them. They exchanged the loving, holy Lord God for demonic, pagan deities.

Hosea went as far as to say that the priests fed on the sins of God's people, that is, they profited from sin (verse 8). When a person sinned, that individual would bring a sacrifice to the priest at the pagan shrines. The priest would get a portion of that sacrifice for himself. Why should the priest worry that people were sinning when it put food on his table? Like an undertaker in the midst of a plague, their business was thriving. They did nothing to stop the people from pagan worship. Their concern was not for the Word of the Lord or for the holiness of the people, but for themselves alone.

Verse 9 tells us that the Lord would judge these priests because of their sin. It did not matter that they were priests. God's sentence would not be any lighter because they were his chosen servants. They would be treated like the common person. They would pay for their evil deeds.

The whole nation suffered from a deep lack of knowledge. God's blessing was removed from the land. They ate but never seemed to have enough. They continued in their prostitution but did not increase in number because God took away their fertility. All this was happening because they had turned their backs on God. They chose wine over the Word of God (verse 11). They chose pleasure over the knowledge of God.

In their wandering from God, his people had stooped so low that they preferred a stick of wood to the true God. They

**Accusations against the Priests** ● 109

rejected the Creator of the universe and the God of their fathers to serve worthless idols.

They were led by a spirit of prostitution. They were unfaithful to the God of their fathers. They sacrificed to foreign idols (verse 12). On the mountains, hills, and in the shade of the trees in the forest, there was evidence of their spiritual prostitution. The people worshiped wherever it was convenient for them instead of in the designated temple area at Jerusalem.

Immorality prevailed in the land. The wives and daughters gave themselves to adultery and prostitution (verse 13). Their men consorted with harlots and shrine prostitutes (verse 14). Here God stated that he would not punish only one party in adultery. He would not punish adulteresses alone without also punishing the men who were guilty with them (see John 8:1–11). Prostitution and drunkenness were rituals in the worship of Baal. God would give idolaters over to their immorality. They were a people without understanding. In their spirit of prostitution, they had rejected God and would come to ruin.

We see how far Israel had wandered from the truth. The whole land was sick with sin. From the priest to the common person, all were guilty before God of forsaking their sacred covenant. They were guilty because they had rejected God and the knowledge of his Word. The priests were not teaching the Mosaic law, but had turned to idol worship themselves. The people had turned their backs on the truth and had given free reign to their sinful lusts and desires.

The land was in moral chaos and would "come to ruin" (verse 14). Although the northern kingdom would be destroyed, God promised in chapters 2 and 3 to restore another generation of Israelites to righteousness. The nation's sins were horrendous, but God was going to do a gracious work in her again. He would bring Israel back to himself by removing the rebellion in her heart. Israel did not deserve God's mercy, but she would receive it by grace.

Maybe today you too are wondering how it could be that God could ever forgive you for the things you have done. No one really knows why God would ever forgive a sinner. The fact is, however, that he does. This is all you need to know. Run to his loving arms, repenting of your sins and praising him for his grace and forgiveness.

*For Consideration:*

- Review the accusations of God against his people. How does your own nation measure up in light of this list?

- To what extent do you feel that the blessing of God is removed from your land today because of sin?

- What needs to take place to stop this trend in your own society?

- What comfort do you take from the fact that the Lord God is willing to forgive us despite the depth of our sin against him?

- What does this passage teach us about the importance of the Word of God in our personal lives and in the world? How has God's Word changed your life?

*For Prayer:*

- Take a moment to pray for your spiritual and political leaders. Ask God to enable them to positively impact your nation for the Lord.

- Pray that God's Spirit would move and bring revival to our needy lands.

- Thank God for his patience with us. Thank him that he is willing to forgive us of all our sins if we repent and call on the name of the Lord.

- Thank the Lord for the impact his Word has had on your life personally.

# 19
# Bad Company

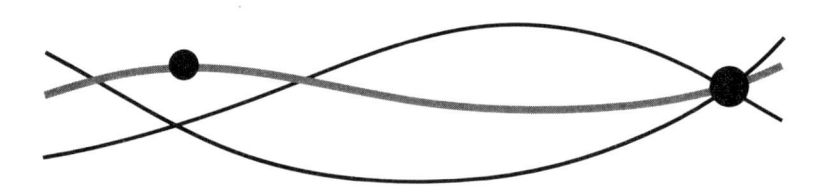

*Read Hosea 4:15–19*

God compared Israel in this passage to a stubborn heifer (verse 16). She had rebelled against the Lord and wanted her own way. God wanted to be her shepherd and care for her, but she rejected his love. Her sister Judah was closely watching Israel's bad example and being tempted to follow her ways. While God warned Judah not to be like her sister, Judah fell into the same trap as Israel.

We cannot underestimate the influence of others in our lives. We are influenced by the company we keep. God understood this temptation in the life of his people when he warned Judah not to go to Gilgal. The town of Gilgal was very important in the history of God's people. It was at Gilgal that Israel first camped after entering the Promised Land. There they reaffirmed their covenant relationship with God by circumcising all the males who had been born in the wilderness and by celebrating the first Passover in the land (Joshua 4:19–20; 5:8–12). Using Gilgal as his military base, Joshua conquered the entire region of Canaan. This location symbolized the victory of God over Israel's enemies. It was here that Israel saw the fulfillment of the promises of God to give them a land of their own. Gilgal was temporarily used as a worship center for the Lord (1 Samuel 10:8) but later became a center for idol worship (Amos 4:4). This once-great city turned its back on God and became known for its wickedness.

Listen to what Hosea would say about it in Hosea 9:15: "Because of all their wickedness in Gilgal, I hated them there. Because of their sinful deeds, I will drive them out of my house. I will no longer love them; all their leaders are rebellious." God did not want Judah to go to Gilgal because of its wickedness. He challenged Judah to stay away from those places where she would be tempted to sin. What a challenge this is for us today. There are places we should not go as believers. Going to these places will only serve to draw us away from the Lord.

God also commanded Judah not to go to Beth Aven. The name *Beth Aven* means "house of deceit or wickedness." While there was an actual location named Beth Aven, nothing of significance is recorded in Scripture as happening in this town. This has led commentators to believe that this name was used by Hosea because of its meaning. God's people were challenged not to go to the "house of wickedness." They were to separate themselves from evil companions and live for God.

God warned his people in verse 15 not to swear any longer by his name. By making oaths in the name of the Lord God when they refused to live for him, they were guilty of blasphemy. God rejected their hypocrisy. Whereas, once he had told them to take oaths in his name (Deuteronomy 6:13), he forbade this practice when it was mixed with idolatry.

In verse 16 God declared that Israel refused him as Shepherd. Although the nation needed his protection, God would leave her as a lamb in the wilderness (see Matthew 23:37). Hosea told his readers that the people of Ephraim had joined themselves to idols. (Ephraim was the largest tribe in the northern kingdom and was often used as a name for this part of the divided kingdom.) The northern kingdom was to be

**Bad Company** ● 113

left alone. This is an expression of God's judgment of wrath in which he turns stubborn sinners over to their own choices (see Judges 10:13; 2 Chronicles 24:20; Psalm 81:11–12). Ephraim was corrupt. Even when all the drinks were gone, the people continued in their prostitution (verse 18).

Alcohol is sometimes used as an excuse for sin. Some people say such things as, "I didn't know what I was doing because I was drunk." Ephraim could not use this excuse. The nation knew full well what it was doing, and did it anyway. Ephraim's rulers did nothing about this evil. They loved shameful ways. Those who should have guided God's people into the way of truth led them deeper into error. Because of Israel's sin, God would send a whirlwind (verse 19). This whirlwind would come in the form of the nation of Assyria, which would sweep them away from their land and take them into exile. Despite an outward show of religion, Ephraim would be brought to shame.

In this passage God called his true people to separate themselves from those who were not living for him. He reminded his faithful that they were a unique people called by his name. As his people, they were to remain holy and avoid places of evil.

*For Consideration:*

- How much do you feel the church of our day is influenced by the secular world? Give some examples.

- Why do you suppose it is so easy to get caught up in the influences around us? How can we avoid getting caught up in sinful practices?

- In what way has your faith been influenced by the people and things around you? Give examples.

*For Prayer:*

- Ask God to forgive you for the negative influence you have had on others.

- Ask him to help you to have a positive influence for the gospel on those around you.

- Ask him to protect you from the negative, unspiritual influences you see around you today.

# 20

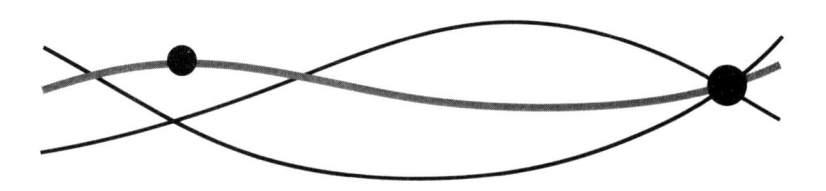

# Guilty!

*Read Hosea 5:1–15*

Chapter 4 showed God's people standing before their Judge. One accusation after another was brought against them, and they had no defense. They knew they were guilty of breaking the divine law, and they awaited their sentence. The great Judge took his place. God called the priests, members of the royal family, and citizens of Israel to hear the sentence he would pronounce on the nation. They listened in silence as God rendered his judgment.

His people were guilty on two counts. First, they had been a snare at Mizpah (verse 1). According to Judges 20, Mizpah was where Israel engaged in civil war with the tribe of Benjamin. This took place because wicked men among them had raped the concubine of a visiting Levite priest. Israel was horrified that such an act should be committed in their land. In just a few days, the tribe of Benjamin was nearly wiped out by the other tribes for this crime. Verse 2 presents us with the imagery of this great slaughter.

Archaeological digs have unearthed idols of the fertility

goddess Astarte in the region of Mizpah. This would indicate that those who were so quick to judge their brothers would themselves fall into sin. The very town that stood so firmly against evil bowed the knee herself to idols. She was being accused of setting a snare for others.

Second, God accused his people of being a net spread out on Tabor. History indicates that the summit of Mount Tabor very likely housed a pagan shrine in the days of Hosea. The imagery is of a hunter spreading out a net on the mountaintop. Like the unsuspecting bird that flew by, God's people were being caught in this net of sin and spiritual adultery.

They could not hide their sin from God. He knew all about their spiritual prostitution (verse 3). He watched as they rejected his Word and became entrapped in the net of sin. He grieved as they gave their hearts and minds to the enemy. They were led by a spirit of religious prostitution (verse 4). There was no more room for God in their lives. They no longer recognized God or acknowledged him (verse 5). They became a proud and self-sufficient people. God removed his blessing and presence from their land. While the idolatrous and hypocritical people continued to offer sacrifices and to practice their religious festivals, God had withdrawn himself from them (verse 6). God would devour them because of their blasphemy. Sin spread like a cancer throughout their nation. They were unfaithful to the Lord, and their children grew up as pagans (verse 7).

A war cry went out to the cities of Gibeah, Ramah, and Beth Aven (verse 8). They were to sound the warning trumpet to alert God's people of the coming judgment. Benjamin was to be on his guard. His neighbor to the north (Ephraim) was going to be laid waste (see verse 9). Judgment for Ephraim meant that the enemy was also close to Benjamin. God would pour out his wrath on Benjamin as well for sins similar to those of Ephraim. Benjamin and Judah made up the southern kingdom, and they were guilty as well of turning away from the covenant. By moving boundry stones, they had broken God's law and dishonestly seized territory that was not theirs. God would pour out his wrath on them for this (verse 10).

Ephraim would be oppressed and trampled by God on the day of punishment because he was intent on going his own way (verse 11). Like a moth, God would eat away his blessings (verse 12). Like rot, God would destroy his inheritance in Judah. Like a ferocious lion, God would attack both Ephraim and Judah (verse 14). In his anger he would rip all Israel apart. In the day of God's judgment, there would be no one to save God's people. Ephraim would run to Assyria for help, but to no avail (verse 13). Assyria would not be able to heal God's people of what was essentially a spiritual problem. Only God could heal them, but they refused to turn to him.

By their persistent rebellion, they had driven God from their midst. God would leave them and return to his place until his people admitted their guilt and sought his face (verse 15). Only then would they recognize just how much they needed him. Their misery would cause them to run back to God and seek his face. There would be a day of revival and renewal for God's rebellious people.

God disciplined his people to draw them to himself. He withdrew his presence from them in grace so that they would see their need of him and repent. He is a long-suffering God. His discipline may be harsh, but it is not final. He is a jealous God. He will not share his people with another god. He loves them too much.

*For Consideration:*

- How many problems in our society are the result of our driving God from our midst?

- If what we are experiencing in our society is a spiritual problem, what needs to take place for our society to be restored?

- What do we learn here about the wrath and discipline of God? Have you ever felt his discipline? Explain.

- God accused his people of driving him away. How did this happen? Are there indications of his presence being withdrawn from us?

*For Prayer:*

- Ask God to open the hearts and minds of people in your nation to see that Christ alone is the solution to national problems.

- Thank the Lord that he loves us enough to discipline us and draw us back to himself.

- What are the sins of your nation? Take a moment to pray that God would touch your nation and draw it to himself.

# 21

# False Piety

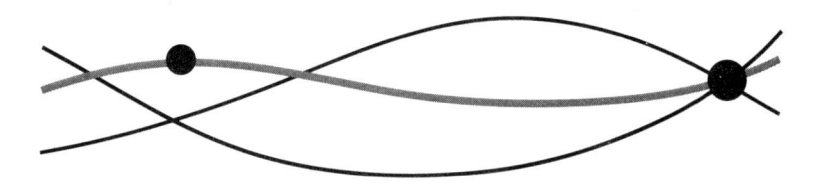

*Read Hosea 6:1–11*

When we lived overseas, we became somewhat familiar with the tropical fruit that grew all around us. I was always amazed to see how quickly the papaya trees in our yard grew. One of the things I noticed, however, was that there were certain papaya trees that never seemed to produce fruit. These trees would grow tall and healthy but appeared to be destined for a life of fruitlessness. Israel was like this. She had all the outward signs of health, but she bore no spiritual fruit.

God had often called his people to repentance. They had heard his voice many times. Notice their response to God: "Come, let us return to the LORD," they said. God's mercy and grace appeared to have no limit. Though God had torn them to pieces, they believed he would heal them. Though he had injured them, he would bind up their wounds (verse 1). They had suffered under the heavy hand of God's discipline, but God did not take pleasure in inflicting them. There was a purpose in what he was doing. The pain and hurt were to force them back to him. God injured them in love. As long as their bellies were full, they would continue in their rebellion. God's people believed that he would come to them in revival in two or three days, that is, very quickly.

In verse 3 the call went out to acknowledge God and to press on to know him better. This requires submission to his will. This is a daily struggle for the believer. Acknowledging God also involves recognizing God's hand in all that takes place in our lives. We should accept his hand in both the good and the bad of life (see Job 2:10). To acknowledge God, therefore, is to live for him and to recognize and praise him for his daily intervention in our lives. Pursuing the knowledge and presence of the Lord is our full-time obligation. God's people were called here to take action in acknowledging God.

God's people believed that God would visit them. As surely as the sun rose in the morning, so God would return to his people. In Hosea 5:15 God told them that he would leave them. God's people believed that he would be right back among them again. He would come to them as surely as the spring or winter rains would bring renewal and refreshing.

All of this talk might seem to us to have been very sincere. God's people spoke here about returning to God and acknowledging him. They spoke of renewal and revival. They spoke the right words. They said the right things, but they could not fool God. When God looked at their hearts, he saw something very different. While these people honored God with their lips, their hearts were far from him (Isaiah 29:13).

"Your love is like the morning mist, like the early dew that disappears," God told his people in verse 4. The morning mist, like the early dew, lasts only for a short while. When the sun comes up, the mist and the dew disappear. This was what the love of God's people was like. It was not a love that would endure. It was very fleeting.

Notice second that God would do to them what they had done to his prophets. He would cut them to pieces. He would kill them with the words of his mouth. This judgment would come like lightning, in great speed and blinding power. Their fancy religious talk would not fool God. He looked beyond their outward appearance to the attitude of their hearts.

Despite their rebellion God's people had not stopped being religious. They continued to offer sacrifices and speak of religious things. Burnt offerings were multiplied in the land. Like the papaya tree mentioned earlier, they looked very healthy on the outside. Their offerings, however, had lost their significance.

In verse 6 Hosea told his people that God desired mercy and not sacrifice. He desired acknowledgment rather than remorse. Sacrifices and offerings were being presented to God by people who neither loved him nor their neighbors. These people showed no mercy to those around them. Mercy is kindness shown to the undeserving. It seems that God's people were offering sacrifices when they were not in right relationships with their neighbors. Maybe they did not think that their neighbors deserved compassion, but this is what mercy is all about.

Jesus told his disciples in Matthew 5:23–24 that if they came to the temple to make offerings and remembered that their brother had something against them, they were to leave their gift at the altar and be reconciled with him before worshiping before the Lord. And here in the Hosea passage, God condemned his people for coming to worship him when they had refused to show mercy and compassion to their fellow citizens. They went through the motions of religion, but they did not have hearts that were in tune with God's commands regarding societal relationships.

God had entered a covenant agreement with these people. He had kept all his promises, but God's people had refused to keep theirs. They were unfaithful to God after he had given them everything they needed. Like Adam they turned their backs on God and his blessings and were unfaithful to him (verse 7).

The Israelite town of Gilead was a city filled with wicked men. It was stained with footprints of blood because of the violence that was taking place there (verse 8). Marauders would lie in ambush, and murder had become quite common in the land (verse 9).

The priests were as guilty as the common people. According to verse 9, the priests murdered and committed other shameful crimes to advance their own interests. They had no fear of God in their hearts. The road to Shechem was the road that connected Samaria, the capital of the northern kingdom, to the pagan religious center of Bethel. Here these priests openly practiced idolatry.

When God looked on his people, he saw a horrible thing. He saw how Ephraim had given herself to prostitution (verse 10). She had turned her back on the Lord her God. She gave her heart to another lover. She was defiled in her lust for other gods and broke her covenant vow with God. In verse 11 the Lord reminded Judah that she also would have a day of reckoning because of her sin.

God wanted to restore his people and forgive their sin. He wanted to see them live in his blessing. The problem, however, was that his people refused to be healed. They loved their sin too much. They persevered in rebellion. For this reason they could not be healed. Their sins had blocked the blessing of God. They spoke well and looked good on the outside, but they produced no spiritual fruit. They would be judged for their hypocrisy.

*For Consideration:*

- Israel spoke the right words, but she was far from God. Could this be true of the church of our day?

- What do we learn here about the grace, mercy, and patience of God?

- God looks at the heart. Why do you suppose we think we can keep sin hidden in our hearts?

*For Prayer:*

- Ask God to help you see things as he sees them. Ask him to help you to move beyond words to sincere character and actions.

- Thank him for his patience with us despite our shortcomings and failures.

- Ask him to enable you to bear fruit for him today. Ask him to show you where you have failed and confess this to him.

# 22

# Israel's Crime

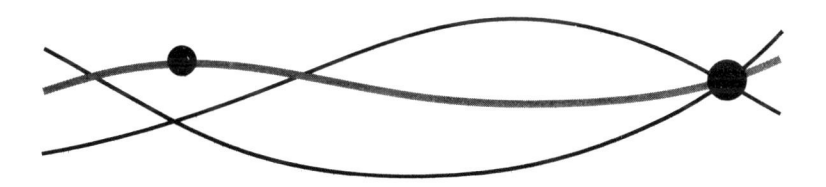

*Read Hosea 6:11–7:16*

The apostle James compared the Word of God to a mirror. A mirror shows us what we are really like. Sometimes we are surprised at what the mirror reveals about us. In this section God set his people in front of the mirror of his Word. They would be confronted with the harsh reality of their sin. Let's look with them into this mirror.

As we begin it is important that we understand that God wanted to heal his people of their sin and evil. At the end of verse 6:11 and in 7:1, he told them clearly that whenever he was ready to restore their fortunes and heal them, new sins were exposed. The love of God's people for their sins and their refusal to repent and deal with these sins kept God's healing from them. God would not bless them in their disobedience. In chapter 7 Hosea exposed the crimes of his people.

God's people did not hesitate to lie, cheat, and deceive others to promote their own personal interests. In regard to honesty and integrity, they were no different from the pagan nations. They could not be trusted. People were not safe even in the confines of their houses in Israel. Thieves would break in and steal their possessions. They could not walk down the street without fear of bandits robbing them.

God saw every crime they committed. He reminded his people: "I remember all their evil deeds. Their sins engulf them; they are always before me" (verse 2). Nothing is hidden from an all-seeing God. He saw every sinful action they committed.

The leadership of Israel in Hosea's day delighted in evil (verse 3). They did nothing to promote righteousness in their nation. In fact, they themselves committed shameful acts. Righteous people had no recourse in the government if they wanted justice because there was too much profit and pleasure in wickedness.

In verse 4 God compared his people's sin to a fire that did not need to be stirred in order to remain hot. Normally, a baker would carefully watch his fire to be sure it would not go out while he was baking his bread. This was not the case for God's people. The flame of their adulterous passion for evil burned brightly. It did not need to be stirred. It smoldered all night and still burned brightly in the morning.

Those who should have been setting good examples for the people joined them in sinful activities. Verses 5–7 describe a plot against a king. Historically, four of Israel's final six kings were assassinated (2 Kings 15). The princes became drunk with wine and joined hands with mockers. These mockers shook their fists at God in word and deed. They had no reverence for the principles of godliness or for the authority of the king. They all lived for the pleasures of the moment and cared nothing for eternity.

The result of this ungodliness was that the leaders were being devoured. They no longer commanded the respect of the people. They ignored the principles of God's Word, and, one by one, they fell from power. God's blessing could no longer rest in their reigns. Even though God had removed his blessing, Israel's rulers refused to call on his name. They chose to die in rebellion.

God's intention was that Israel be different from the surrounding nations and separate herself from their sinful practices. She had been chosen of God and was the object of his special attention (Exodus 19:3–6). She was to be a light to the nations and an ambassador to the world (Isaiah 49:6). She had fallen short of her great calling. She had chosen to mix with the nations and soon became just like them.

What was the result of her mixing with the nations? God compared this result to the cooking of flat cakes or pancakes (verse 8). While cooking a pancake, it is important that it be turned over so that both sides are cooked. When a pancake is not turned over, the result is that one side is burned and the other is uncooked. When this happens the pancake is spoiled and cannot be eaten. This is what had happened to Ephraim. Her mixing with the nations had destroyed her usefulness to God as a blessing to the world (see Genesis 12:3). On the one hand, she appeared to live for God, and on the other, she lived for the world. Like the pancake burned on one side and uncooked on the other, Ephraim was completely ruined.

God's presence in her midst was Israel's strength. Her association with these nations, however, had driven God's presence away. These nations were causing God's people to turn from the principles of his Word. The result was a weak and anemic people devoid of spiritual strength and vitality.

God's people were becoming old before their time (verse 9). Even as physical strength diminishes with age, so these people were losing their spiritual strength and vitality. The worst part about it all was that they did not realize what was happening to them. They did not even notice that they were drifting away from God and becoming weak and helpless. Historically, Israel paid large amounts of money to Assyria and Egypt for alliances, but these nations eventually betrayed Israel (2 Kings 15:19–20; 17:3–6).

How subtle the enemy works in our lives. He saps our strength ever so slowly. We may not even notice the change. One day we take a good look in the mirror and notice how old and sickly we really are. Our love for God is no longer alive and fresh. We find ourselves helplessly trapped in sin. We wonder how we arrived at this point. God's people had given in to the enemy one temptation at a time. Now they were helplessly trapped.

Israel's great sin was arrogance (verse 10). Someone has said that pride is the center of all sin. This was the sin of Israel. She refused to humble herself and return to God, her only protector. The people of Israel were blind to what was happening. The nation was dying by becoming enslaved to other nations, but the people did not realize the seriousness of the situation. They believed that foreign alliances would protect them against their enemies. What they did not know was that the allied nations were their enemies.

God compared Ephraim to a senseless dove (verses 11–12). The dove is one of the easiest birds to catch. This is what Ephraim was like. Without discernment she would fall into any trap the enemy set. One moment she would turn to Assyria and her sinful ways as a source of strength, and, at another moment, she would turn to Egypt. God would discipline Israel for the sin of turning away from him. He would spread out his net and draw her down to the ground.

God's people had strayed from him. They had been fascinated by the sins of the nations around them. Like wandering children whose curiosity got the best of them, the people of Israel refused to listen to the voice of God warning them about the dangers ahead. The result of their wandering and rebellion was devastating (verse 13).

Despite their rebellion, the Lord God longed to bring Israel back to himself. His arms were wide open to receive them, but they refused to return. Instead, they told lies about him. We are not told what these lies were. We do understand, however, that there were false prophets in Israel who spoke their own word in the name of the Lord. This may be in part a reference to these individuals. Were these false prophets telling the people of God that everything would be all right when in reality things were very wrong? What is clear is that God's people refused to hear and speak the truth about God. Their denial of the truth kept them from experiencing his blessing.

God's people wailed on their beds, but they would not cry out to him (verse 14). They knew in their hearts that things were not right, but they refused to do anything about it. They knew that their rebellion was wrong and that they experienced the pain of separation from God, but they loved their sins too much. They refused to repent. Instead, they gritted their teeth and persisted in their sin.

In verse 14 we are told that Israel assembled for grain and new wine (a sign of God's blessing), but they turned from God. They wanted the best of God's blessings and, at the same time, the pleasure of their sin. They could not have both.

God was the source of their strength. They owed every breath to him. He had instructed them in the way he wanted them to live, but they refused his way. Instead, they used the very strength he gave them to rebel against him (verse 15).

In the final analysis, they refused the Most High. They turned their backs on the great God of this universe who loved them. They were like a faulty bow that missed the mark (verse 16). They could not be trusted with God's blessings. Their leaders would perish and the nation would be ridiculed and mocked.

God showed his people through Hosea what they were really like by placing them in front of the mirror of his Word. You cannot read this section of Scripture without seeing the broken heart of God. "What can I do with you, Ephraim?" he asked in Hosea 6:4. "Your love is like morning mist, like the early dew that disappears." God wanted to restore their fortunes, but their sins were in the way (7:1). He longed to redeem them, but they spoke lies about him (7:13). How rebellious they had become.

Maybe you too are like Israel. Maybe today you need to see afresh the grace of God. In the midst of your sin, he calls out. He longs to redeem. He longs for intimacy with you as his child. What sin is holding you back? Ask him to help you yield your heart to him today.

*For Consideration:*

- What does this section teach us about the patience and long-suffering of God?
- Why is it important that we let the Word of God be our mirror?
- What does this passage teach us about how sin blocks the blessing of God in our lives?
- What is the heart of God for his children? What kind of relationship does God want with his children?
- Review the list of accusations against God's people in this section. Which of these accusations apply to our own society? Which apply to you personally? Give specific examples.

*For Prayer:*

- Take a moment to pray for your nation. Ask God to deal with some of the particular issues you are facing today.
- Thank him for his patience with us even when we have wandered away from him.
- Ask God to reveal any sin in you that he wants to deal with today. Ask him to cleanse you and draw you into a deeper relationship with him.

# 23
# Fruitless Faith

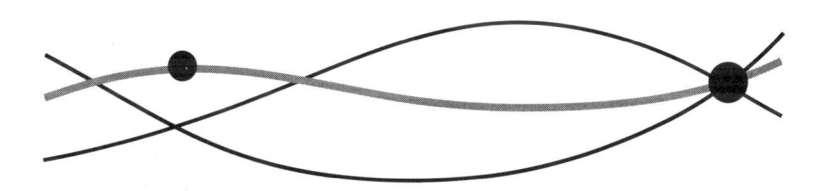

*Read Hosea 8:1–14*

At the beginning of chapter 8, God called for the sounding of the trumpet. The trumpet was sounded in ancient times to warn of an approaching enemy. The enemy in this case was represented as an eagle. The eagle is a bird of prey. It flies over its victim and swoops down to devour. The eagle represented the judgment of God in the form of the Assyrians who would dive down to devour Israel.

Moses prophesied in Deuteronomy 28:49–52:

> The LORD will bring a nation against you from far away, from the ends of the earth, like an eagle swooping down, a nation whose language you will not understand, a fierce-looking nation without respect for the old or pity for the young. They will devour the young of your livestock and the crops of your land until you are destroyed. They will leave you no grain, new wine or oil, nor any calves of your herds or lambs of your flocks until you are ruined. They will

lay siege to all the cities throughout your land until the high fortified walls in which you trust fall down. They will besiege all the cities throughout the land the LORD your God is giving you.

A day of judgment was coming for the people of God. This is not to say, however, that the people of Israel were not a religious people. In verse 2 they said, "O our God, we acknowledge you!" While they acknowledged God with their mouths, they had rejected what was good (verse 3). Israel's religion had become a useless repetition of words only and not of deeds. The nation perceived itself to be very different from how God perceived it.

In our culture we teach our children to be independent. We feel we have raised them well if they grow up being able to make their own decisions and live their own lives independently of their parents. When it comes to God, however, this is not how things work. The more mature we are spiritually, the more dependent on him we become. Israel was seeking independence from God and wanted to live apart from the Mosaic law. Israel did not consult the Lord when it came to the matter of choosing political leaders (verse 4). God wanted to be involved in the decisions his nation made (see 1 Kings 19:15–16). Israel claimed to acknowledge God, but their actions showed this was not true—they did not consult him for important decisions.

God had blessed his people with great wealth and prosperity. While these things were good in themselves, God accused his people of using what he had given them to make idols. This was another area of life where Israel did not seek the Lord. Israel had failed to acknowledge God in the use of resources. All we have really belongs to God. He alone has the right to do as he pleases with what he has given to us. We need to seek him in how we use our resources. Israel had failed to do so.

Israel's idol was a calf god. A calf-idol had been set up in certain cities in the northern kingdom by King Jeroboam to keep Israel from worshiping the true God in Jerusalem (1 Kings 12:28–30). God told Samaria—the capital city of the northern kingdom—to throw away their calf-idol (verse 5). He reminded them that the day was coming when their idol would be destroyed. They were investing their lives and resources in a false and demonic religious system that had no power to help them or save their souls.

God was very angry with his people for their idolatry. Israel would be punished for this blasphemous disobedience and refusal to acknowledge the God of their covenant. In verses 7–10 God warned his people of the dangers of rejecting him.

Hosea described Israel as having sown the wind (verse 7). What they sowed was blown away by the wind. They were wasting their lives and resources. They were not wisely investing in eternal matters. Israel would stand condemned before God with nothing to show for having been a people in covenant with the all-powerful, all-loving God of creation. Because Israel had sown the wind, Hosea warned that the nation would reap a whirlwind of God's wrath.

God compared his people to stalks with no head. What is the good of a stalk of grain with no head? The stalk cannot be eaten. It is good only to be thrown to the cattle or burned. This was God's description of Israel. The people had become completely useless to the Lord God. There was no spiritual fruit in their lives.

Through continued rebellion Israel had driven the presence of God from her. God used the nation of Assyria to invade Israel and deport the people to various parts of the Assyrian Empire (verse 8). Israel alone was to blame for this. She had turned from the Lord for protection and gone to other nations to form alliances (verse 9). Israel was tempted by the philosophies and sins of these foreign nations and gradually lost all distinctiveness as a people of God. In the end her enemies swallowed her up, and she wasted away under their oppression (verse 10).

This is very different from what Israel had been under the reigns of King David and King Solomon. Israel had been the envy of every nation on the earth. God's people were feared and revered as mighty and powerful. Then they lost everything and became an oppressed and miserable people, wasting away because they had refused to keep the terms of the Mosaic covenant.

Religion formed an important part of Israel's everyday life. This religion, however, was not a true religion. The temple in Jerusalem was the only proper place to worship; Ephraim had filled the land with pagan altars (verse 11). When the people brought their sin offerings to these altars, they were mocking the Lord and his covenant. These rebellious Israelites performed pagan religious rituals with hearts that were far from God.

Though Israel had received the law of God, this law had become foreign to them (verse 12). They lived the way they wanted and disregarded the commandments of God. The law of God was a stranger in their midst. Like a dusty Bible on a shelf, the law was never consulted. The people did not acknowledge God because they enjoyed the pleasure of their sins.

God refused to accept their sacrifices because they were not offered according to the law (verse 13). Their religion was blasphemous. God saw their wicked hearts and hated their hypocrisy. God would punish the people by returning them to the Egyptian slavery from which he had redeemed them hundreds of years before. However, this time their "Egypt" would be Assyria.

Though Israel had built richly adorned palaces, she had forgotten the Lord God who had provided the prosperity (verse 14). She had become so absorbed in her own interests that she had no time for her Maker. Judah also built fortified towns. She felt that she did not need the Lord God to be her strength. She too had abandoned her Creator.

What would be the result of this self-trust and arrogant sin? God would consume their fortresses. All the strongholds and palaces would tumble to the ground. Israel's day of strength and power would be no more. She would stand naked before God. Her fancy buildings and fortresses would be of no use to her in the day of her judgment.

Here before us is a religious people who are not right with God. They considered themselves to be the people of God, but they did not consult him. They did not invest in spiritual matters. They went through the motions of religion, but their hearts were untouched by the truth of the Word of God. God was not pleased with them. Their impression of themselves differed greatly from God's impression of them. This passage challenges us to consider our own relationship with the Lord. It's not what we think about ourselves that matters but rather what God thinks about our spiritual condition.

*For Consideration:*

- What is God looking for in his people? How does God expect his people to express their relationship with him?

- Do you need God's help in an area of weakness in your life? What is it in particular?

- What does this passage teach us about our need to seek God in all things?

- Take a look at your own life. Is your life fruitful for the Lord? Explain.

- What is the importance of our attitude in the practice of our faith?

*For Prayer:*

- Has the Lord challenged you from this section of Scripture? Ask him to help you make things right in a weak area of your life.

- Ask God to give you a sincere and honest heart before him.

- Thank him for his patience with you despite your many failures.

# 24
# Israel's Punishment

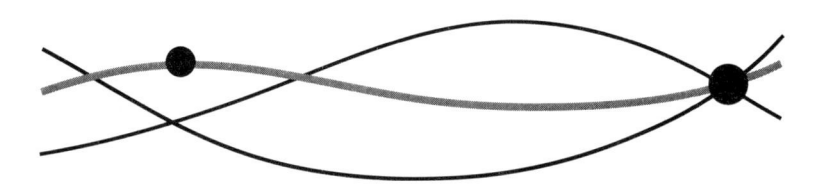

*Read Hosea 9:1–17*

A quick look at the world will show us that the unbeliever lives for temporary pleasures. This is always the philosophy of an unrighteous age. It seems to me that if there were no life after death, we might as well join the world in this pursuit. But there is life after death, and all people will stand accountable to God for how they lived their lives. As God's chosen nation, Israel was not to join in the celebrations of the nations around her (verse 1). What was the reason for this? Did God not want his people to rejoice and enjoy the good things he had provided? The context of this chapter indicates that God's people were forbidden this practice for two reasons.

The first reason had to do with what God's people were enjoying. We saw in the last chapter that the people of Israel were guilty of taking pleasure in their sins and unfaithfulness to God. They had been led astray into prostitution and spiritual adultery. They became attracted to the immorality of pagan religion and lost sight of God and his holy commands. The Canaanites practiced their fertility rites on the threshing floors of the land. In these locations they engaged in immoral sexual practices to ensure the fertility of the earth. Israel joined in these pagan festivities. She too invoked these fertility gods. No longer did she recognize God as the source of the harvest. She was rejoicing in rebellion against God.

The second reason Israel was not to rejoice like the nations was because of what was about to happen. God would remove fertility from the land. There would not be enough crops and wine to feed the people (verse 2). These were covenantal curses that God had promised for unfaithfulness (Deuteronomy 28:38–42). They would lose their land to the Assyrians. They would live in exile, eating the unclean food of strangers (verse 3). They were not to rejoice because they were about to lose everything they had. Their sin and rebellion had brought covenantal curses on them.

Israel was God's chosen nation. She was the object of his special attention. She had received his law. She had been chosen to be a light to the nations. Because of her honored position and knowledge of truth, Israel's crime was more serious than that of the nations. There is an obligation attached to being called by God's name. Israel had failed as God's representative and had blackened the name of God in the eyes of the nations. God would not leave this unpunished.

Similarly, as his representatives, we are to live for his honor and glory. To refuse to do so is to blaspheme the name we represent. This is a serious matter and merits serious punishment. Your sins as a believer and representative of God in this world are not to be taken lightly. You carry his name with you wherever you go.

God was no longer pleased with their religious service. He refused to accept their insincere offerings and sacrifices (verse 4). Because they blasphemed his name, God refused their worship. Their sacrifices no longer pleased him because they were not offered with hearts that were in communion with him. Their sacrifices were like the bread of mourners. The bread of mourners was bread that had been touched by those who had been defiled by a dead body. Because this bread was unclean, it could not be eaten (see Deuteronomy 26:14). The sacrifices the people brought to the temple of the Lord were unclean like the bread of mourners. God did not want these unclean sacrifices. He told them to keep their sacrifices for themselves as food, because he would not accept them.

In verse 5 the Lord asked the people: "What will you do on the day of your appointed feasts, on the festival days of the LORD?" (verse 5). The Assyrians were going to invade their land and deport them. They would no longer be able to properly worship God according to the Mosaic laws. What would they do when their freedom to worship was taken from them?

God's people were guilty and would be punished by God according to their covenant with him. Hosea described the punishment that awaited God's people because of their sin.

Those people that the Assyrians or Babylonians did not capture would go to Egypt, Hosea told them in verse 6. Memphis was an Egyptian city known for its tombs. In the days of Jeremiah, this is exactly what took place. The people who remained in the land after its conquest by Assyria and Babylon decided to take refuge in Egypt. God told them through Jeremiah that they would perish in the land of Egypt because they did not put their trust in him (Jeremiah 42:17).

The land the Lord their God had given their ancestors would be overtaken by thorns and briers (verse 6). The treasures they were forced to leave behind would be stolen or destroyed. The land would become a wasteland. Thorns would overrun their tents because there was no one to cultivate and care for the land.

The sins of God's people were many. They had resisted the Lord God and his purposes for them. They considered God's prophets to be fools and maniacs (verse 7). God had sent many prophets to be his watchmen for the nation. They called the people to repentance and warned of God's coming judgment. But instead of welcoming divine wisdom, Ephraim was hostile to the true prophets and made their ministries very difficult (verse 8).

A day of reckoning was coming for the people of God. God would not forget their wickedness (verse 9). He compared these people to the evil men of Gibeah whose heinous crime was infamous and unforgettable (see Judges 19). Whereas God forgives and forgets all confessed sins, God would remember all these rebellious sins. If God's people did not repent, they had the guarantee of Almighty God that they would receive a just punishment for their iniquity. Nothing short of confession and repentance would stop this judgment from taking place.

Verse 10 is like a rose among thorns. We have seen the terrible anger and judgment of God in the above verses. But here in verse 10 we catch a glimpse of God's heart of compassion and love for his people. When God first chose the forefathers of Israel, it was a time of delight for him, like finding grapes in the middle of a desert. What excitement filled his heart in the early days of the nation. Like a farmer seeing the first fruit on his fig trees, so it was when God saw Israel begin to bud. God loved his people. He took great pleasure and delight in them. His people, however, even before entering the Promised Land, worshiped Baal idols at Peor and became an abomination in God's eyes (Numbers 25:1–5). The smile of God's loving approval was quickly changed into a frown of wrath.

Because his people resisted all efforts to be drawn back to repentance, God had to punish them. Ephraim's glory would flee. Like a bird that takes flight and disappears, so would be the fruit of Ephraim (verse 11). God's blessing of children would be removed, and Ephraim would be left barren and desolate. Ephraim had worshiped the Baals to increase fertility, so God chose infertility as a specific judgment.

Those children who were born would suffer. Many would die and never reach adulthood. Those mothers who did conceive would miscarry or lose their children to the murdering invaders (verses 12–13). Those who gave birth would have dry breasts (verse 14). They would have nothing to feed their children. With

**Israel's Punishment** ● 139

God's presence removed from them, his people would wither up and die. They had forgotten that they owed everything to God. By breaking their covenant with him through gross immorality, they passed the death sentence on themselves.

Verse 15 speaks very powerfully of the intense hatred of God for the terrible sins of his people: "Because of all their wickedness in Gilgal, I hated them there." Gilgal was a center for idol worship and symbolized Israel's spiritual adultery. God was forced to drive Israel out of his covenant house of worship and intimate fellowship. Israel refused every opportunity to return to God. The covenant demanded banishment from his presence and from his affections.

God's people were of no more use to him. They were unfruitful (verse 16). They resisted every attempt of God to be reconciled. They rebelliously chose to follow the ways of the pagan nations around them, which God hated. God had no choice but to turn his back on them and reject them as sinners unwilling to receive his forgiveness. This is not to say that God had forever abandoned his people, the Israelites. Even after Hosea there would be renewed calls from God through the prophets to repent and return to their covenant. The Lord Jesus would come and live among his chosen people, calling them to turn to him for forgiveness and salvation. Scripture teaches that God has not abandoned Israel (see Romans 11:17–27). As for those of Hosea's generation, they would be judged—taken from the land and scattered among the other nations (verse 17; see Deuteronomy 28:62–66).

This passage is a challenge to those of us who belong to the Lord. As his representatives, we have the responsibility to live for him and represent his name for righteousness in all we do. The punishment described in this chapter is very severe, but so is the crime. God's people had forgotten that they were his representatives and that he is the only source of blessing and salvation. Much is required of those to whom much has been given.

*For Consideration:*

- How would you evaluate Christianity today? Are we good representatives of God and his character? What are our weaknesses?

- What comfort do you find in the fact that while God rejected the generation of Hosea's day, he would renew his offer of fellowship to other generations? Do you believe that your generation has been faithful to the Lord God? Explain.

- What sins have driven a wedge between us and God's blessings? If we truly humbled ourselves as believers before the Lord, what blessings would we expect to see?

*For Prayer:*

- Ask the Lord to help you be a good representative of his name. Confess your personal shortcomings, and ask for his enabling in these areas of your life.

- Thank the Lord that he is a just God who will not accept sin and evil. Ask him to search your heart to see if there is any sin that needs to be confessed.

- Thank the Lord for his intense delight in you as his child. Thank him that he considers you like "grapes in the desert."

# 25

# It is Time to Seek the Lord

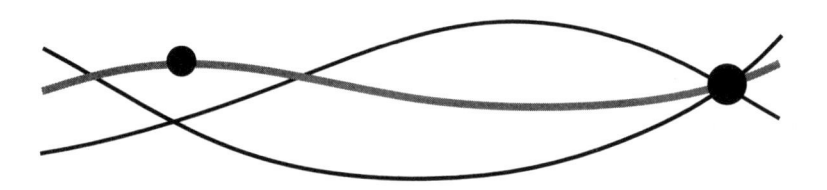

*Read Hosea 10:1–15*

Hosea compared Israel to a spreading vine bringing forth fruit. She grew in number and influence under God's blessing. The problem, however, was that the more she was blessed, the more she fell in love with her blessings instead of the one who blesses. The more her fruit increased, the more she built altars for fertility gods (verse 1). As Israel prospered she adorned her sacred places of idol worship. Israel's blessings should have increased her gratitude to God, but the blessings increased her independence. Prosperity led to spiritual corruption.

The prophet told his people that they were guilty and would pay the price for forsaking the Lord. Their altars and sacred stones would be demolished (verse 2). God told his people that he would destroy the objects that they worshiped. He would justly punish his people for their religious and social crimes against his righteous law. In our lives these altars and sacred stones are those things that draw us away from the Lord.

In the day of God's judgment, his people would have no

one to turn to. Their evil king would not be able to help them when God unleashed his anger (verse 3). Because they had rejected their heavenly king, God would reject their earthly king. The people would see that an earthly king is helpless against God's wrath.

The whole nation was steeped in deceit (verse 4). A person's word could not be trusted. God's people made promises and agreements but did not keep them. Lawsuits sprang up throughout the land as people broke their word with each other. These lawsuits are compared to poisonous weeds springing up in a plowed field. The whole nation was overcome by these weeds of deception. They choked out the blessing of God.

In verse 5 Hosea prophesied that in the capital city of Samaria, the citizens would live in fear when they saw their calf-idol taken from them. They had bowed down to this idol for protection and fertility since their conception as a nation. The Assyrians would invade and take away their nation and their god. Their idol would serve as tribute to the king of Assyria (verse 6). The people of Israel would be ashamed and disgraced because neither their idols nor their foreign alliance with Assyria would help them in their day of trouble.

Samaria, the capital of the northern kingdom of Israel, and its king would be taken away into exile (verse 8). Like a twig taken by the water current, God's people would be helpless against their enemy. Their high places, where they bowed to their foreign gods, would be destroyed. Thorns would cover their altars. God's people would be brought to utter hopelessness. They would despair of life. Hosea told them that the day was coming when they would cry out to the mountains and hills to fall on them so that they could perish and not endure the terrible judgment of God. Jesus used the same words in Luke 23:30 about a final day of judgment.

God's people had sinned against him since the days of Gibeah (verse 9). In Judges 19–21 we see that it was in the region of Gibeah that Israel engaged in civil war against the tribe of Benjamin because of its immorality. Gibeah was a symbol of

It is Time to Seek the Lord ● 143

rebellion against the standard God had laid out for his people. It also was a symbol of slaughter and judgment. It was the place where brother turned against brother.

Hosea warned his people that the Lord God would punish them for their sin. Nations would gather against them. They would be put in bonds for their double sin (verse 10). Jeremiah used a similar expression in Jeremiah 2:13: "My people have committed two sins: They have forsaken me, the spring of living water, and have dug their own cisterns, broken cisterns that cannot hold water." What was the double sin of the people of God? Was it not, first, that they had forsaken God and, second, that they had turned to idols?

Ephraim was compared in verse 11 to a trained heifer that threshed the grain. Threshing was the process by which the grain was separated from the straw. This was done either by beating the straw or by having oxen trample it. According to Deuteronomy 25:4, the ox that threshed was to be permitted to eat as it worked. Obviously, for an ox, this would be a very pleasant task. It could eat all it wanted as it threshed the grain. This was a picture of God's people under God's loving care. They enjoyed the blessing and bounty of God. They were happy to serve as long as they were getting something out of it for themselves. God told them, however, that those days were over, and they would have to wear a yoke (verse 11). They would no longer have the pleasant task of threshing the grain. They would be driven by a plow. Things would be difficult for them because they had turned away from God. No longer would they see the richness of God's blessing. Their daily existence would be one of difficulty and pain.

In verse 12 God called his people to repentance. They had been sowing seeds of sin and self-glorification all their lives. It was time to repent and make some major changes. The Israelites were called to live for the Lord their God and to sow seeds of righteousness. They were challenged to break up the hardened ground of their hearts. In so doing, two things would happen: they would reap the fruit of God's unfailing love, and the Lord himself would pour his showers of righteousness on them. This is a well-known verse and is a good summary of God's ongoing message to his rebellious people.

God promised that if his people humbled themselves in his sight and broke up the hardened ground of their lives, then he would shower righteousness on them. Notice that this righteousness would come from God and that it would be showered on his people. Righteousness only comes after our hardened hearts have been broken. We can never become what God wants us to become until we die to ourselves and our pride. There are those who believe that they have the personal power to live the life God commands. They seek to establish their own righteousness. God promised to shower his righteousness on those who would humble themselves before him. This is not something we do for ourselves. Righteousness is a work of God in us. It is not what we do for God but what he does for us.

What was the response of Israel to this pleading of God? In verse 13 we read that she continued to plant wickedness. Israel turned her back on her God and the righteousness he promised to give her. Because she planted wickedness, she reaped the fruit of wickedness in her land. The seeds of evil produced a crop of deception and wickedness throughout the country. Israel did things in her own way. She was not interested in the principles of God's Word, and she would reap what she had sown.

Israel trusted in her own strength. She did not see her need of God. She felt she was big enough to make up her own mind and fight her own battles. She would soon find out how much she needed God. God would rise up against her, and her fortresses would be devastated (verse 14). Hosea reminded his people of a past event when they had been overwhelmed because they had not trusted in their God. He reminded them that their children had been dashed to the ground by the cruelty of an enemy.

There was no future apart from God for the nation of Israel. Hosea warned them that they were on the wrong path. The path they walked led to devastation and death.

The warning is clear to us as well. We cannot afford to ignore what God is telling us through his Word. To turn our backs on God is dangerous. The warning goes out from the lips of the prophet Hosea. He challenged his people to break up their unplowed hearts and soften them toward the things of God. He called them to repentance and righteousness. It was not too late. If they turned to their God, he was willing to shower them with his righteousness.

*For Consideration:*

- What is the difference between a righteousness that comes from God and our own efforts to be right with God?

- Do you think that we often live by works, seeking to merit God's favor? What is the difference between serving the Lord to merit his favor and serving out of a heart that overflows with gratitude?

- There were those in Hosea's day who served God only for what they could get out of him. Is it possible for us to fall into this same sin today?

- What are the blessings promised in this section of Scripture to those who humble themselves before the Lord?

*For Prayer:*

- Take a moment to thank the Lord that his righteousness is showered on all who will humbly come to him. Thank him that he gives us his righteousness.

- Verse 8 reminds us of the terror of those not living for the Lord when he returns. Take a moment to pray for someone who does not know the Lord. Ask God to reveal himself to that person.

- Ask God to examine your motivation for serving him. Ask him to give you a pure and holy motivation to serve him out of love and devotion.

# 26

# Grace in Rebellion

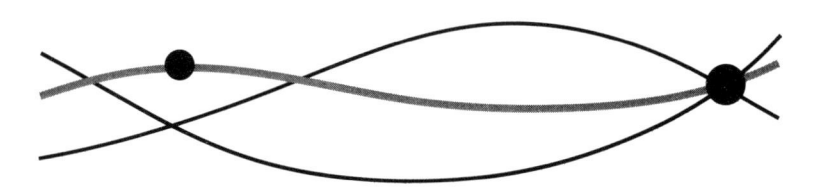

*Read Hosea 11:1–12*

Have you ever shared one of those moments with your family where you reflected on the fond memories of the past? Maybe it was the moment your first child was born. Maybe it was the loss of a first tooth. There are many happy memories stored away in our minds. This is something of what the Lord God is doing here in this chapter.

God took his people back in time to the beginnings of Israel as a nation. He compared Israel to a young child dearly loved by a father. God told of how he, with great care, took Israel out of the land of Egypt and was proud to call him "my son" (verse 1).

The joy of verse 1, however, was quickly turned to grief, because this son did not love his father (verse 2). The more God called his son to come to his side, the more Israel ran from his father. Israel was not interested in learning the ways of his loving father. There were so many sinful things to see and do. Israel turned from the one true God to false gods and began sacrificing to the Baals (see Deuteronomy 8:14–20).

God's heart was broken by the rebellion of his child. "It was I who taught Ephraim to walk," (verse 3). He had taken Israel by the arms to keep him from falling. He had picked Israel up when he fell and brushed off the dirt from wounded knees.

God always led his child with kindness and love. Hosea reminds us in verse 4 of how God took the yoke off Israel's neck and bent down himself to feed him. The picture here is of an individual feeding an ox. In order for the ox to properly eat, the owner would take the yoke off its neck. God not only took off Israel's yoke but also bent down to feed and care for him. This is the role of a servant. God's love and kind service never lacked toward his son Israel.

Despite God's great compassion toward his people, they consistently turned their backs on him. The result was that they would be driven from his presence. They would return to captivity and bondage (Egypt) from where he had rescued them (verse 5). Assyria would rule over them. The sword would flash in their city, breaking down their gates (verse 6). The great plans they had for themselves would come to an end under the judgment of the Lord. All this would happen because they insisted on wandering away from the Lord. They were determined to follow the path of rebellion (verse 7). God would not answer cries from insincere, wicked hearts.

Despite their rebellion, God's love remained solid and unmoved (verse 8). His heart churned within him as he considered his judgment of Israel. "How can I give you up, Ephraim" he asked. "How can I hand you over, Israel?" While God had every right to treat his people like the cities of Admah and Zeboiim, it brought him great pain. According to Deuteronomy 29:23 these two cities were destroyed along with the cities of Sodom and Gomorrah: "The whole land will be a burning waste of salt and sulfur—nothing planted, nothing sprouting, no vegetation growing on it. It will be like the destruction of Sodom and Gomorrah, Admah and Zeboiim, which the LORD overthrew in fierce anger."

While the anger of the Lord should have prevailed, it was

his compassion that was stirred. He chose not to carry out his fiercest anger (verse 9). God has fierce anger against sin because of its devastating effects on the things he loves. Let us never doubt this for a moment. Here, however, we see that he is also a God of unmerited favor toward sinners. Unlike humans, God's extends his grace to those who have hated him and blasphemed his name. Although God would bring covenantal punishment against Israel, God would finally show his loving kindness again to his chosen nation.

This did not mean that God would ignore the sins of Hosea's generation. They would know his stern discipline. He would roar like a lion (verse 10). In so doing, he would call his children to account for their actions. But the day was coming, however, when God would pour out a spirit of repentance, and his trembling nation would return to him in repentance. "They will follow the LORD."

Verse 11 tells us that God's people would come like birds from Egypt and doves from Assyria. Could this be a reference to the swiftness with which they would return to him? The dove is a bird of peace and is a very timid bird. This is also how God's people would come. While they would come to him in swiftness, they would, like a timid dove, be fully aware of their sin. When they came to the Lord in this manner, they would experience his renewed blessing. They would again settle in their homes and know the smile of God on their lives. Some commentators believe that verses 10–11 refer to a future restoration of Israel to faithfulness to the Lord.

In Hosea's day God's people were quite happy to live in their rebellion and not seek him. Ephraim surrounded God with lies and deceit. Judah was an unruly child and resisted her heavenly father (verse 12; some versions translate this verse differently). God was always faithful to the covenant with his people, and he punished them according to his promises.

Ultimately, he would pour out a spirit of repentance in the midst of their rebellion. Instead of completely destroying them as they deserved, they would be forgiven and restored to a right relationship with their God. Like a good shepherd, God would chase after the wandering sheep. Out of love for his people, God blocked their path lest they be completely overcome by sin. Praise God who watches over his people and never breaks his promises.

*For Consideration:*

- Have you been aware of God's grace and mercy in your life in recent weeks? Give an example.

- What evidence do you see in this section that proves that God takes great personal interest in you as his child?

- Do you have any reason to believe from this section that God would ever abandon you? Why?

*For Prayer:*

- Thank the Lord for the evidences of his grace and love toward you. Thank him that his love for you never changes.

- Ask God to pour out a spirit of repentance on your land.

- Ask God to help you to love and forgive your friends and neighbors, as he has done for you.

- Take a moment to thank the Lord that he is such a forgiving God. Thank him for forgiving you.

# 27

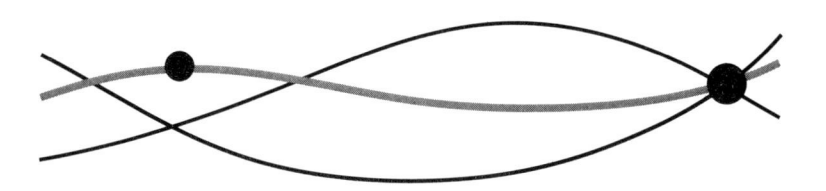

# More Sin

*Read Hosea 12:1–14*

Have you ever experienced claustrophobia? What happens when you begin to feel enclosed by space? Everything inside you screams for release. Every nerve in your body is on edge. I wonder what God felt when he found himself surrounded by the things he hated most, sin and deceit. In the last chapter, we saw that the people of Israel were surrounding a holy God with their sin and evil (11:12). Everywhere God looked, there was sin in the land. What would stop him from lashing out in anger and righteous indignation?

Ephraim was feeding on the wind (verse 1). Have you ever caught the wind in your hands? Can the wind provide nourishment for the body? This is a picture of futility. God's people were wasting their time and energy pursuing evil. In the end, all their efforts would bring the opposite of what they hoped for. They could not compete against God's love and righteousness.

Lies and violence were on the increase in the land of Ephraim. What they could not get by lying, they would take by violent means. Principles of honesty and respect had been cast aside. Greed and pride ruled in contrast to the integrity and humility commanded in God's laws.

God had promised to be their strong tower (Psalm 61:3). Everything they needed they could have found in him. What an honor and privilege it was to be his children. Nothing could harm them under his protection. They had everything they could ever have hoped for and more. God's people, however, were seeking military protection from other nations. They entered into a treaty with Assyria and sent oil to Egypt to enlist her support.

How willing God is to reach out to us in our need. His unending resources are at our disposal. How often do we claim those resources? If we were honest, we would probably find ourselves as guilty as the people of Ephraim. When we have nowhere else to go, we turn to God. How this must grieve him. A missionary friend once said, "It's not that we don't pray, it's that we don't make it the first thing we do." How often do we wait until we are backed into a corner before going to God? How much pain and agony we would avoid if we made prayer and seeking God our first step.

God's people had turned to others. In so doing, they had turned away from God and broken the terms of the covenant. God would repay his people according to their deeds (verse 2). Even as a child in the womb, their forefather Jacob had grasped his brother's heel (Genesis 25:26). Throughout the lives of Jacob and Esau, there was bitterness and deceit between them. This bitterness was passed on to the descendants of Jacob and Esau. Jacob was a self-seeker, and this attitude drove him to struggle with God. In pride Jacob would take on anyone who stood in his way.

Not all of Jacob's grasping was bad. His natural perseverance caused him to seek a blessing from an angel after a long fight with him (Genesis 32:24–26). Jacob refused to allow the angel to go until he had blessed him. Hosea told his listeners that Jacob begged for the favor of God with tears (verse 4). God answered his desperate, humble prayer and blessed Jacob.

**More Sin** ● 153

The problem, however, was that Jacob's strong point was also his greatest weakness. While his aggression did cause him to struggle *for* God, it would at other times cause him to struggle *against* God. At this point in their lives, the people of God were struggling against their Creator. They needed to return to him as Jacob returned to Bethel and heard God speak (Genesis 35:14). The Lord God of Jacob is the Lord of hosts, the Lord Almighty who controls all the powers in heaven and earth (verse 5). This was Israel's God, whom she had deserted.

Hosea called Israel to return to the Lord Almighty (verse 6). Like Jacob, Israel had forgotten love and justice. As we have already mentioned, Jacob was born grasping the heel of his brother, which was symbolic of his life of self-interest and deception. The people of Israel abandoned the social laws of the covenant, and love and justice were cast aside in pursuit of individual interests. In verse 6 Hosea called his people back to God's righteous laws, just as Jacob had returned to God after years of deceptive ways. God's people needed to learn to humbly wait on God's will in God's time. That meant that they were to seek their God in all things. They were to learn not to run ahead of God and his plan, grasping in self-interest as Jacob had done.

We have already seen that love and justice had been forgotten in the pursuit of personal interests. Honesty and integrity were also cast aside (verse 7). The merchants of the land used inaccurate scales to cheat and defraud their customers. This did not go unnoticed by God.

Dishonesty and fraud did make them wealthy. In fact, Ephraim boasted of wealth and felt secure in worldly possessions. The people believed that their money could protect them. They thought that they could buy their way out of any problem.

In verse 9 God reminded his people of the days when they came out of Egypt. In those days they did not have fancy houses but lived in tents. They did not own property but roamed from one place to another in the desert. In those days they were entirely dependent on God for their daily sustenance. While the Israelites to whom Hosea was presently speaking had not themselves experienced this wandering in the wilderness, they had heard about it and commemorated it by living in tents at certain times of the year (Leviticus 23:42–43). God reminded his people that they would once again live in tents like their forefathers. The day was coming when they would be stripped of their fancy houses and land. In that day of judgment, they would be forced to depend on God one day at a time.

God had warned his people, through the prophets, of a coming judgment, but they would not listen (verse 10). He sent prophets with visions. They spoke to God's people in parables so that they could understand, but they were not interested in God's word. These people were not sinning out of ignorance but in direct defiance of God's spoken word.

The city of Gilead had become a very wicked city (verse 11). Its citizens were useless to God. In Gilgal their pagan altars were multiplying throughout the land. A day of judgment was coming. On that day their altars would be pulled down and piled like stones on a plowed field. Their false gods would be useless to them on the day of God's judgment.

When Jacob deceived his brother by stealing his birthright and blessing, he was forced to flee his homeland to save his life. Out of grace God cared for him in the land of his exile, but he had to work hard to pay for his wife (verse 12). Later in the land of Egypt, under the heavy oppression of Pharaoh, God graciously sent a prophet named Moses to rescue his people (verse 13). He delivered them by signs and wonders and gave them a land of their own.

You would have thought that his people would be eternally indebted to God for his goodness to them when they and their forefathers had been helpless. But this was not the case. Ephraim had bitterly provoked the Lord to anger (verse 14). Israel, who had been showered with kindness, became guilty of the foulest of crimes. She who had received God's grace from her earliest origins repaid him by showing contempt for his

More Sin ● 155

name. God would not leave the guilty unpunished. He would hold them accountable for their actions and return them to slavery in foreign nations where he had found them.

We owe our lives to God. We have been given and forgiven much, and we owe him much in return. He has rescued us from hell. He has given us life in Christ. What a horrible thing it is to turn our backs on him.

What can we offer in return for all he has done for us? Let us who have been forgiven much love much (see Luke 7:47). Let us cast aside personal interest and self-gratification. Let us give ourselves wholly to him who gave himself for us. Anything short of this is sin.

*For Consideration:*

- Compare God's people here in this section to your own society on the following terms: 1) masters of their own destiny, 2) striving after the wind, 3) self-sufficiency, 4) stepping on others to promote self, and 5) materialism and dependence on wealth not God.

- What causes us to wander from God? Are there any particular areas in which you have been guilty of wandering from God?

- What do we learn here about the love, compassion, and justice of God?

- Have you ever been caught in the trap of dependence on the things of this world and not on God?

*For Prayer:*

- Ask the Lord to reveal any area of your life in which you are not seeking him. Ask him to give you grace to repent and seek him.

- Thank the Lord for his mercy and compassion even when we stumble and fall.

- Do you know someone who has been wandering from the Lord today? Take a moment to pray that the Lord would restore that person to himself.

# 28
# Rebellious Ephraim

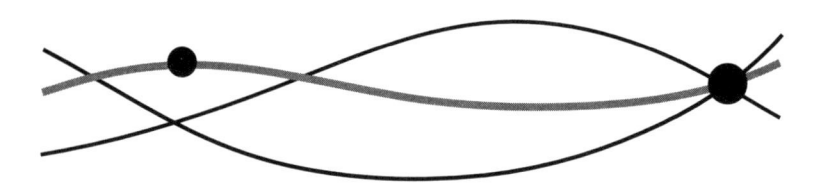

*Read Hosea 13:1–16*

Of all the tribes of Israel, Ephraim was the greatest. Ephraim was the largest tribe, and when Ephraim spoke people listened. Ephraim had authority among the people of God and was an exalted tribe (verse 1). When the nation of Israel split into two kingdoms, the ten northern tribes were often referred to as Ephraim. God had poured out his blessing on these people.

What was Ephraim's response to this wonderful privilege and blessing of God? They turned their backs on God to serve Baal (verse 1). Ephraim led the other tribes into Baal worship, and this sin brought with it the seeds of spiritual and national death. When the people turned to idolatry, they died. They died to their usefulness to God, and they died to their relationship with God. They also died physically as a nation. God eventually punished his nation with destruction.

As time went on, Ephraim and the other Israelites became more and more entangled in sin (verse 2). Their craftsmen took pride in fashioning idols of silver. They even offered human sacrifices (2 Kings 16:3; Jeremiah 32:35). They kissed the calf-idols, thus showing their reverence and love for that which God hated. The people of Israel became like the nations around them. Their witness and testimony for the Lord God was destroyed. They were indistinguishable from their unbelieving neighbors. They lost all love and desire for the true God and his holy laws. Their hearts went after demonic gods. How this grieved God who had created and chosen them as his own.

God would not sit idly by and watch his people continue in sin. God compared them to the morning mist and the early dew that disappeared. As great as they had been, they would be no more. Israel would cease to exist as quickly as the disappearing dew in the morning sun. The nation would be blown away like the chaff swirling around on the threshing floor. God's people would offer no resistance. They would be helpless before the wind of God's fury and would disappear like smoke escaping through an open window (verse 3).

God had always cared for his people. When they were being oppressed and beaten by the Egyptians, God reached out and saved them (verse 4). He brought them out of the land of their slavery. He guided them through the desert (verse 5). When they were hungry, he fed them (verse 6). For forty years he provided for their every need as they wandered through the wilderness. Never once had he failed them. Because they were well cared for, they soon became proud. In their pride they forgot who fed them. They forgot that without God they were nothing. They forgot that behind their greatness was the grace and mercy of a loving and gracious God.

God would deal with his unfaithful people in his fury. He would pounce on them like a lion. Like a leopard stalking its prey, God would be a constant threat to them (verse 7). They would pay the price for their rebellion. God would attack them in fury, like a mother bear robbed of her cubs (verse 8). Like a lion, he would devour them. Like a wild animal, he would rip them to pieces. They would be destroyed because they turned their backs on their covenant God and only helper. "You are destroyed, O Israel, because you are against me" (verse 9).

In the day of God's wrath, their kings would not be able to save them (verse 10). Many years ago they had cried out to God for a king. They told the prophet Samuel that they wanted to be like the other nations (see 1 Samuel 8). God did not refuse them this request. While this was not his desire for them, their stubborn insistence pushed God to teach them the hard way. The Lord gave them a king in anger. They learned that their dependence on a human king, instead of the Lord alone, brought them only sin and destruction. In the day of God's judgment, where were these human protectors? What could they do for God's people in their day of divine wrath?

There is a lesson for us here. There are times when God will give us over to our stubborn wills. He calls us to live in obedience, but, if we persist in disobedience, he may turn us over to our evil desires to learn the hard way. In the end we will suffer loss.

Hosea told his readers in verse 12 that Ephraim's guilt had been stored up. God's people had piled one sin on another. God had not stopped them. They had the responsibility of choice in this matter. While God did not stop their sin, he did keep a record of all their wrongs that served as evidence against them. They would one day give an account of their actions to God.

In verse 13 Hosea compared God's discipline of Ephraim to childbirth. Through these birth pains of discipline, God had been calling his child to leave the comfortable womb of sin. The Lord, as the mother, was also in pain trying to bring forth this child to new life, but Ephraim refused to hear God's voice. He refused to come to the opening of the womb, and so he would perish.

Directly following the strong rebuke of Ephraim in verses 12 and 13, God again announced in verse 14 his strong love for his chosen people and his promise of a future deliverance. The fulfillment of this promise may be seen in Israel's restoration from exile, in the redemption of Christ and his kingdom, and in individual restoration from death to glory. In the New

Testament Paul used this verse to speak of the resurrection of believers (1 Corinthians 15:55). God always promises that those who receive his discipline in faith will be rescued from the power of the grave. God will not forsake us in our final trial. Not even death will defeat believers because we hope in God, the author of life. However, God has no pity on the unrepentant. On them he "will have no compassion."

Despite these promises Ephraim refused the discipline of the Lord. Hosea told God's unfaithful people that an east wind would blow over them from the desert. Assyria was located to the east. The Assyrians would plunder Israel, looting their storehouses and their treasures (verse 15). Samaria, the capital of the northern kingdom, would suffer the full consequences of rebellion against God. The people would fall by the sword. Their little children would perish as they were dashed to the ground. Their pregnant women would be ripped open by the sword of their enemy (verse 16). Their devastation would be terrible.

A horrible picture of judgment was presented to God's people here. We will not understand this chapter without remembering that God is holy and must judge sin. This chapter, however, is also filled with hope. We are also presented here with a loving God. He is the God who rescued his people from the bondage of Egypt. He is the God who provided for their every need as they wandered through the wilderness. He is the God who delighted in exalting his child Ephraim. He is the God who promises victory over death. In him there is blessing beyond measure. Outside of him there is only judgment and wrath.

*For Consideration:*

- Consider for a moment the fragility of life. Can you think of a practical example of how someone, in an instant, lost all they held dear?

- What keeps God from removing his blessings from us and our society?

- Give an example of how the pain of God's discipline drew you closer to him.

- What does this passage teach us about the hardness of human hearts and the lure of sin?

- What do we learn here about the love of God for his people? What does the passage teach us about the holy justice of God?

*For Prayer:*

- Thank the Lord for his blessings. Name a few of them.

- Are you going through a trial right now? Thank the Lord that he promises to work this out for your good.

- Thank the Lord for how he has drawn you closer to himself through trials.

- Ask the Lord to give you a heart that is sensitive to him.

- Do you know someone who has wandered away from the Lord God? Take a moment to pray that the Lord would draw this person back to himself.

# 29

# The Conclusion of the Matter

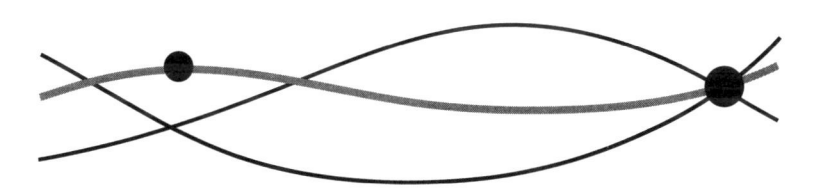

*Read Hosea 14:1–9*

**W**e come to the conclusion of this prophecy of Hosea. The list of sins has been accumulating from chapter to chapter. The wrath of God has been revealed. God's people remain stubborn in their resistance against the Holy One of Israel. Listen to God's final word to this prodigal nation.

In verse 1 God called his people to return to him. After all they had done, the door was still open for them to return to their covenant relationship with the Lord through repentance and obedience. God's people had sinned grievously against him. Their lack of repentance had been their downfall. God had not abandoned them and was still their God. He still wanted them to return to him, and his arms were open wide to receive them. His grace seems to have no limit. His love for his people is constant and unmerited.

In verse 2 Hosea challenged his people to approach God boldly and ask him to receive them. This would have been a real step of faith for those who had been guilty of so much sin and rebellion. Notice here that God required that they ask for forgiveness. Too many people expect that they will be forgiven without asking. We should never assume this.

Hosea told his people in verse 3 how they were to approach this holy and just God. He told them first to come to God realizing that he was their only hope. He told them to confess that Assyria could not help them. Assyria was a dominant world power of the day, so it was a real temptation for the people of God to run to Assyria for help. God required that his people recognize that no one else could protect them. He required that they put their full confidence and trust in him alone.

The second step of repentance is also found in verse 3. Here God told his people to admit their sin and turn from it to follow him alone. He wanted to hear them say that they would never again place their faith in pagan gods. They were to give their full attention to the God of Israel. He alone was to be their God. He wanted his people not only to recognize that they had been wrong but also to turn from their sins, never to return. They were never again to say, "Our gods," when looking at the work of their own hands. In other words, they were never again to make or worship idols.

This did not mean that they needed to be perfect before they came to God. God promised in verse 4 to heal their backsliding and to love them freely. This is important. They could not heal their sinful ways through self-effort. They needed to come to the Lord for healing. God would shape them into his image when they returned to him. They were to come with a repentant and willing spirit, but it was God who would have to make them into the people they needed to be.

All too many people think that they have to be perfect for God to accept them. This is not the case. God accepts us as we are and shapes us into what we should be. The Lord is looking for those who recognize their sinful ways. He is looking for those who desire to turn from sin to him. We come as we are. We come with our sin and waywardness and place it at his feet. God is in the business of healing sinful hearts. What joy it should give us today that God wants to give us victory over the sins that enslave us. God promised his people in verse 4 that he would turn his anger from them and love them freely. All they had to do was confess their sin, recognize God as their only hope, and come to him for healing.

If Israel came and sought his face, God promised to be like the dew (verse 5). In chapter 6 God compared the love of his people to the dew that disappears quickly in the morning, but here a different picture was intended. Although the dew disappears quickly, it has a very positive effect on the earth. The dew waters and refreshes the earth. This is what God was saying to his people. He was telling them that he would be like dew on a parched earth. He would come to them to refresh and bring vitality. The result would be that the nation would again blossom like a lily and a cedar, sending down roots deeply into the earth. Israel would become beautiful, strong, and a blessing to others (verses 6–7). The fragrance of God's people would spread throughout the earth.

What was it that kept God's nation from experiencing this prosperity? In verse 8 Hosea announced that it was idols. God's unfaithful people could never experience divine blessing with idols in their lives. Turning from God's laws had led them only to despair and hopelessness. God was offering them fruitfulness and prosperity. If they would turn from their false gods, God would be like a great tree for them. The tree was used for construction purposes and is here a sign of prosperity and blessing. God wanted his people to enjoy prosperity again. He wanted their homes and lives to be rebuilt. He wanted them again to flourish, but their idols prevented this.

"Who is wise? He will realize these things," Hosea told his readers in verse 9. The ways of the Lord are right, and the righteous will walk in them. Throughout this book God called his prodigal nation to himself. We have seen how real his wrath is against those who persist in evil. We have also seen how he pleaded with his people to return to him and experience his forgiveness. Wise people will hear this call and give themselves to seeking God with all their hearts. On these wise people, the blessing of God will be poured out in abundance.

*For Consideration:*

- What does this final chapter tell us about God's desire for his people?

- How does God want us to approach him?

- What does this section teach us about God's desire to give us an abundant life? Do you presently experience this abundance? What keeps you from it?

*For Prayer:*

- Ask God to help you to experience the full life promised to his people here in this section. Ask him to help you to become aware of those things that keep you from that fullness.

- Thank the Lord that he is a God of rich blessing and infinite mercy.

- Do you know someone who is wandering away from God? Take a moment to pray that the Lord God would draw this individual to himself.

# Joel

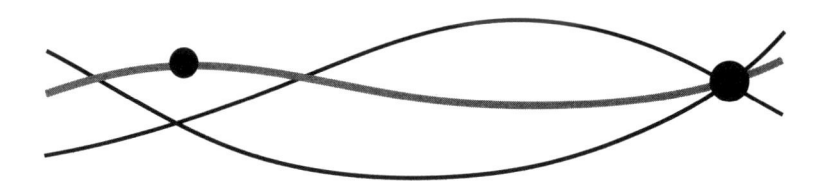

# 30

# Victory in Humility

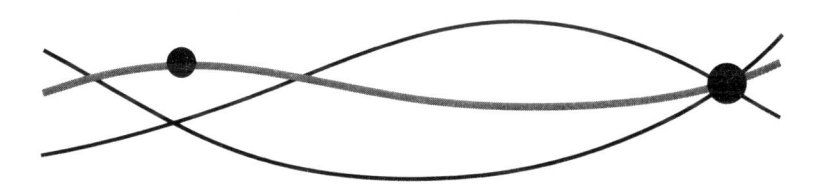

*Read Joel 1:1–20*

This is the prophecy of Joel. His name means "Jehovah is God." Joel was the son of Pethuel of whom we know nothing. In this prophecy Joel described a terrible calamity that had come on the land. "Has anything like this ever happened in your days or in the days of your forefathers?" Joel asked in verse 2. These were times to be remembered. What was Joel speaking about?

Joel went on to describe a great plague of locusts. Verse 4 can be quite difficult to understand. There are four different Hebrew words used in this verse to describe the insects that infested the land. Each of these words refers, in some way, to a locust. The first word is *gazam*. This word is translated in the KJV by the word "palmerworm." A palmerworm is a locust in its caterpillar stage. The word comes from a root word meaning "to devour" and describes the action of the locust at this stage of its growth cycle.

The second Hebrew word used is *arbeh*. It refers to a locust in its grasshopper stage. The word comes from a root word meaning "to multiply" or "to increase rapidly." The third word in verse 4 is *yeleq*. This word is translated in the KJV as "cankerworm." The cankerworm is a young locust at yet another stage of development. It is believed that at this stage the locust would not have yet developed wings. The Greek translation of the Old Testament (called the Septuagint) translates this word as "unwinged locust."

The final Hebrew word used here for locust is *chaciyl*. The KJV translates this as "caterpillar." The NKJV seems to capture the sense of this verse best when it reads, "What the chewing locust left, the swarming locust has eaten; what the swarming locust left, the crawling locust has eaten; and what the crawling locust left, the consuming locust has eaten."

Joel was describing a major plague of locusts. These locusts had infested the land, coming in swarms, laying their eggs, and devouring the vegetation. In time the eggs hatched, and the young larvae emerged. In turn, they devoured what their parents had left behind.

How serious was this plague of locusts? Joel turned his attention in verse 5 to the drunkards of the land. He told them that they were to awaken from their drunken stupor and weep because of what was taking place in the land. The vines had been taken from them. There would be no new wine in the land. The locusts had taken the wine from their lips.

The locusts were compared to a great nation invading the land of Israel (verse 6). They were so numerous they could not be counted. They were powerful and destroyed everything in their path. They had teeth like a lion with which they devoured the vines and fig trees. They stripped the bark off the trees of the land and left the branches white and dying.

The whole land mourned. Joel called on the people of the land to mourn like a virgin whose future husband had been taken from her (verse 8). The priests were to mourn because the grain and drink offerings had been cut off from the house of the Lord (verse 9). There was nothing to offer to the Lord because the locusts had consumed the crops. All the fields were ruined (verse 10). The grain, the new wine, and the oil had failed. The farmers and vine growers were called to mourn because the wheat and the barley harvest had been destroyed (verse 11). The vine and the fig tree had withered, as had the pomegranate, palm, and apple trees (verse 12). All the trees of the field were dying, having been stripped by this great army of locusts. There was no cause for rejoicing in the land at the normal time of harvest. Joy had been replaced with despair because the land lay in ruins.

In verses 16-20 the prophet continued with this theme of devastation. It appears from these verses that the plague of locusts was only part of the problem. There had been no rain in the land, and drought had caused erosion. All the food had been cut off (verse 16). Joy and gladness were removed from the house of God. The planted seeds shriveled up beneath the surface of the ground. The storehouses were in ruins. The grain that remained in the granaries was dried up and useless (verse 17). The cattle moaned and were slowly starving to death. There were no pastures for them to feed on (verse 18). Though innocent, the animals suffered tremendously under this heavy discipline of the Lord (see Romans 8:18-22). Fire devoured the dried pastures and burned the trees of the fields (verse 19). The wild animals panted and perished for lack of water. The streams in the land had dried up (verse 20).

The picture before us is one of utter desolation. The hand of God had been removed from the land. The proud people of Judah had been humbled under divine discipline. God had threatened locust plagues if his covenant people proved unfaithful (Deuteronomy 28:38, 42). God's disloyal people were helpless to do anything to stop this righteous judgment. They are held completely at the mercy of a holy God. Why had this taken place? Was there any hope for God's people? Verses 13-15 give us some answers to these questions.

Through his prophet Joel, God called the priests to put on sackcloth and to mourn and wail (verse 13). They were invited to spend the night before the Lord their God at the temple in

Jerusalem. As spiritual leaders of God's people, they were asked to proclaim a great fast (verse 14). The elders and people of the land were to gather for this solemn occasion. On that day they were to humble themselves and call out to the Lord their God. The day of the Lord was near, and it was a day of destruction from the Almighty.

What did this fast represent for the people of God? It represented their recognition that they were helpless before the enemy. Abstinence from food and other pleasures rendered them physically and emotionally weak, symbolizing that they did not need human strength for this battle. If victory was to be theirs, it would not be in their personal power. In this weakened and urgent condition, they were to come to God sincerely pleading for *his* strength and enabling.

A great spiritual victory is won when we humble ourselves and recognize our need of God. We do not gain God's approval by inflicting ourselves with pain and suffering in our abstinence from food. We do not fast so that God will take pity on us and grant our request. The great value of fasting is found in what it accomplishes in us: it shows us how weak and frail we are. This weakened state is an affront to our pride and self-dependence. It reminds us of our limitations and causes us to look to Almighty God. It also reminds us that victory is not in our human strength but in the Lord God, who delights in coming to the aid of the humble and meek. The apostle James tells us in James 4:6: "But he gives us more grace. That is why Scripture says: 'God opposes the proud but gives grace to the humble.'"

Hope of victory for these Israelites would not be found in themselves. They had to come to a point were they realized that their hope was in God alone. God's people could do nothing to change their desperate situation. They could not hold discussions with the locusts. They could not make it rain. No amount of human wisdom or strength could remedy their circumstance. Only in God could they find victory. Sometimes God will bring us to the end of ourselves to show us how much we really need him.

*For Consideration:*

- Have you ever forgotten how much you need God and are dependent on him? Why is it so easy to trust in your own strength and wisdom?

- What "locusts" do you have to deal with today? What is it that strips you of spiritual blessings today?

- Why is it so hard for us to recognize our total dependence on God?

- What role did repentance play in the restoring of God's blessings to his people? What do we need to repent of today?

*For Prayer:*

- Confess any attitude of pride that this passage may have revealed in you.

- Recognize before God how frail you really are. Praise him for the blessings he has given you today.

- Thank the Lord that he is willing to restore our blessings if we come to him with repentant hearts.

# 31

# The Approaching Army

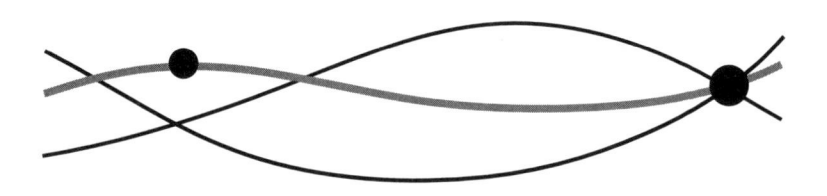

*Read Joel 2:1–11*

A terrible thing was about to happen in the land. The trumpet of warning was to sound in Zion. This was a day for fear and trembling. The day of the Lord was coming. This day would be a day of wrath and judgment. It was a day of great darkness and gloom, blackness and clouds (verse 2). Like dawn spreading across the mountains, a large army was advancing toward God's people. Never before in the history of the nation had they seen such a massive and powerful army. Never again would they see such a mighty force. Some commentators believe that Joel used a recent locust plague (chapter 1) as a metaphor and warning of a coming greater devastation from the Lord—the invasion and capture of Judah by the Babylonians.

As this great army moved, fire went before it, devouring everything in sight (verse 3). In front of the army lay the paradise God had given his people (referred to here as the garden of Eden). As the army moved through this paradise, it devoured everything and left behind a desert wasteland. Nothing escaped destruction. What was this great army that approached the people of God? The context of an army of locusts continues in chapter 2.

These locusts had the appearance of horses (verse 4). Joel compared them to horses because of how they advanced. They galloped like horses in a cavalry. Have you ever seen a charging horse? It comes with great speed and is intent on destruction. These locusts approached with the speed and intent of a charging war horse.

The locusts were compared to a horse also because of the noise they made. A person could hear them coming. The noise of their approach was like an army of chariots rushing into battle. In verse 5 Joel compared the swarming locusts to the sound of an approaching fire consuming everything in its path.

There is a third reason why these locusts were compared to horses. This reason has to do with the way they could leap over the obstacles strewn on their pathway. When there is an obstacle in front of a horse, it leaps over it and continues its path. Nothing hindered the approach of this army of locusts. They flew over entire mountains as they approached the people of God.

At the sight of this great army, the nations were in anguish (verse 6). Their faces turned pale with fear. Nothing would stop these creatures. They charged like warriors. They were not distracted from their course but marched straight ahead. When walls were in their way, they simply climbed the walls. They broke into the city of God. They ran along the walls of the city of Jerusalem. Like thieves, they broke into houses and helped themselves to whatever they desired (verse 9). By virtue of the enemy's strength, the people of God were helpless against this attack.

What is most surprising here is the person who is at the head of this great invasion. Verse 11 tells us that the Lord God himself led this great force. As he moved the earth shook and the sky trembled. The sun and the moon were darkened as the Lord moved out in judgment of his own people. No one could resist the Lord and his great army. The forces at his disposal were beyond number. Each of his soldiers was mighty and powerful. This was a terrible day for the people of God. Their own God had turned his hand of judgment against them. There was nothing they could do to stop it.

What do we learn from this passage? The first thing we need to remember is that each of us, like the children of Judah in Joel's day, was guilty before God. We were his enemies by virtue of our sins. We were the objects of his great wrath and judgment. He was marching against us, and we could do nothing to oppose him. His strength and power are beyond our ability to resist. To all appearances, like Judah facing the invasion of locusts, we too were doomed to destruction. As rebellious sinners, we were at the mercy of a holy God who hates sin. Were it not for the Lord Jesus, who became our mediator and provided a means whereby God and humankind could be reconciled, we would have all perished under the wrath of God (Ephesians 2:1–5).

The second thing we need to be reminded of here is that those who were under God's judgment in this passage were the people of God. Don't think that because you are a Christian you will not have to answer to God. The Lord Jesus said that "men will have to give account on the day of judgment for every careless word they have spoken" (Matthew 12:36). The apostle Paul told the church in Corinth, "If any man builds on this foundation using gold, silver, costly stones, wood, hay or straw, his work will be shown for what it is, because the Day will bring it to light. It will be revealed with fire, and the fire will test the quality of each man's work. If what he has built survives, he will receive his reward. If it is burned up, he will suffer loss; he himself will be saved, but only as one escaping through the flames" (1 Corinthians 3:12–15).

The apostle Paul also challenged the church in Rome not to take their relationship with the Lord for granted. "You will say then, 'Branches were broken off so that I could be grafted in.' Granted. But they were broken off because of unbelief, and you stand by faith. Do not be arrogant, but be afraid. For if God did not spare the natural branches, he will not spare you either" (Romans 11:19–21). Paul spoke of how God's people of the Old Testament period were cut off because of their unbelief. We who are under grace and have the knowledge of the Lord Jesus Christ are under an even greater obligation today. If God disciplined his people in the Old Testament, will he not do the same today?

As children of God, we are accountable to him for our actions in a way the unbeliever is not. As his children, we have the greatest obligation to live for him and serve him. It is a serious thing to turn our backs on the Lord who saved us. There is more damage caused to the work of God by believers who persist in sin than there is from the unbeliever. The writer to the Hebrews warned his readers in Hebrews 10:28–29 about treating the blood of Christ that sanctifies them as unholy: "Anyone who rejected the law of Moses died without mercy on the testimony of two or three witnesses. How much more severely do you think a man deserves to be punished who has trampled the Son of God under foot, who has treated as an unholy thing the blood of the covenant that sanctified him, and who has insulted the Spirit of grace?"

The prophet Joel called for the trumpet to be sounded in Zion. It was a warning to the people of God as the Lord advanced against his own people because they had turned their backs on him. Let us take heed to the warning given to the people of God in the days of Joel so that we too don't fall under the Lord's strict judgment.

*For Consideration:*

- For what sins do you feel the church of our day will be judged by God?

- Take a moment to consider where you stand personally before God. Are there things you need to make right before him?

- Why should we be thankful that God is a God of holy judgment?

- How did the Lord Jesus save us from the wrath of God?

*For Prayer:*

- Thank God that even though this chapter describes the judgment each of us deserves, there is forgiveness in Christ.

- Ask God to strengthen you to live for him as he requires.

- Ask God to renew his church before it becomes the object of his great judgment, like Judah.

- Take a moment to thank the Lord that he is a holy and just God who will punish sin.

# 32
# Return to Me

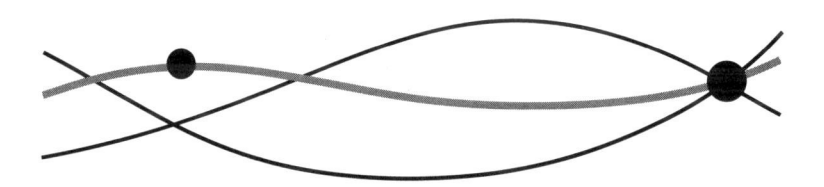

*Read Joel 2:12–27*

One of the tremendous truths of the Christian faith is that despite our rebellion, there is always forgiveness and acceptance in the Lord if we confess our sins. No matter how far we have wandered, through the door of repentance God will receive us with open arms. We catch a glimpse of this compassion and patience of God in this section of Joel. After warning his people of the dangers to come, God then called them to return to him. His love for them was constant and unconditional.

"Even now," declared the Lord, "return to me" (verse 12). Even though the enemy army was on its way, it was still not too late. The offer of forgiveness and restoration was still open. God did not take delight in judging his people.

Notice in verses 12 and 13 how God's people were to return. God demanded that they return to him wholeheartedly. He expected them to return with fasting and weeping. What did this fasting and weeping represent? It represented their repentance and great sorrow for sin. As they came to him, they needed to recognize their sin. Their hearts were to be broken because of their rebellion against the Holy One. Joel told his people in verse 13 that God was not at all interested in their outward show of religion. They were to rend their hearts and not their garments. It is easy enough to put on a great show of repentance. This would fool people, but it would not fool God. God was not at all interested in their heartless demonstrations of piety. If they came to him, it would have to be with a sincere heart.

Repentant Judah could return because God is a God of compassion and graciousness. He is slow to anger and always full of love. He does not delight in sending calamity and judgment. It is in his character to forgive. This would only take place, however, if his people truly were remorseful for their sins. Even as the enemy army was approaching, if the people returned to God with all their hearts, he might yet have pity on them (verse 14). In his sovereignty and grace, God could still avert his judgment and give his people a blessing. From a plentiful harvest they would be able to offer grain and drink offerings, as offerings of thanksgiving and praise to the Lord who controls all things in his world.

A call went out in verse 15 to the entire land. Everyone was to come to a solemn assembly. An invitation was extended to the elders, as the political and spiritual leaders, as well as the children and nursing babies. Even the newlyweds who would normally have been excused from such assemblies (Deuteronomy 24:5) were to be present that day. No one was exempt.

As they gathered before the Lord, the priest was to lead them in a prayer of repentance. Notice in verse 17 that the priests were to weep between the temple porch and the altar. The fact that they were to weep indicates that they should be broken-hearted by their own sins as well as those of the people. They could not lead the people of God in repentance if they themselves were not repentant. The porch of the temple was where the common people would gather. As they gathered in the great porch of the temple, they stood before the altar of the Lord. It was there that sacrifices were made for the sins of the people. The altar was a constant reminder that the punishment for sin is death. As they stood before this altar of sacrifice, the priest was to beg God to spare his people, though their sins had been great and merited his wrath. With tears, the priests were to plead with God for forgiveness and grace for themselves and the people.

Joel told Judah what the response of the Lord would be toward those who truly repented in this way. He told them in verse 18 that God's jealousy would be incited for his people. His heart would be moved by their genuine tears of repentance. He would have pity on them and pour out his blessings on the land. Beginning in this verse, God's people cease being the object of his wrath, which is then turned on the approaching enemy army.

The repentance of God's people would restore the productivity of the land. If God's people truly returned to him, they would see a great healing of their nation (verse 19). The Lord would bless their crops. His people would be satisfied fully with his abundant blessing. Nothing would be lacking. Never again would they be the scorn of the nations but would become the envy of their neighbors.

In verse 20 Joel told his people that if they repented, God would drive away their enemy. The great army of invaders would be pushed back into a barren land and into the sea. The stench of their decaying corpses would rise into the air, and God's people would be freed from their oppression.

Peace and security would return to the land. There would be no cause for fear. The wild animals would no longer perish (verse 22). The trees and the vines would again produce their fruit. The inhabitants of the land could live in security and peace because the Lord their God would provide for their every need. God's people would have every reason to rejoice and be glad. The rains would come in their time. Farmers would again come with their grain to the threshing floors. The wine vats of the land would overflow with an abundance of new wine (verse 24). God's blessing would be showered on them as a people, and they would rejoice in his goodness.

God would restore to them all the years the locust had taken prosperity from them (verse 25). It was as though the blessings withheld while they were living in sin were being stored up in their account for the day of their repentance. On that day the storehouses would be opened and this accumulated blessing would be poured out on them. God did not need to make up for the years the locust had taken from his people. His people were guilty of sin and had paid the price for that sin. Covenant curses had come because of sin; covenant blessings would come because of repentance (Deuteronomy 28).

God mercifully gives to his people what they do not deserve. We can take great courage from this verse. Have you wasted years of your life? Are you ashamed of what you have done? He can multiply the fruit of your righteousness in the years that remain. Your life can still count for something. He can use the years that remain in ways you never thought possible.

Notice finally that God would restore praise and thanksgiving to the land (verse 26). Once again a right relationship would exist between God and his people. Their hearts would be full of gratitude and worship for the Holy One of Israel who forgave them of their sins and worked wonders in their midst. They would know that the God of Israel is the one true God and that there is no other god beside him. They would have great reason to lift their heads high. When they were restored to a right relationship with God, they would have no reason to be ashamed (verse 27).

What a contrast this section of Scripture is to the last section. In verses 1–11 Joel spoke of devastation and hopelessness. Here in verses 12–27 we see hope and blessing. God was presenting his people with an option. They could choose either blessing or cursing. The only thing that separated them from the blessing of God was repentance. Their sin had separated them from God. It had driven a wedge between them and the blessings God wanted to pour out on them. (See Deuteronomy 30:19–20.)

What sin separates you from experiencing the full measure of God's blessing in your life today? Spiritual prosperity, peace, security, gladness, and thanksgiving can be your present experience. The key is repentance and turning from sin. Take a moment now to consider what it is that hinders you from experiencing this fullness in your life today. Confess that sin, and let God heal the hurt and pour out his blessing on your life.

*For Consideration:*

- What blessings would you expect to see in your land if its inhabitants turned from sin to serve God?
- What is it that keeps your nation from turning to God?
- Is there anything that keeps you from experiencing God's full blessing today?
- What does this passage teach us about the grace and forgiveness of God?
- What do we learn here about the importance of our heart attitude as we seek God?

*For Prayer:*

- Thank God for his grace and mercy despite our sin.
- Ask him to bless the years that remain to you. Ask him to restore to you any wasted years you may have lived.
- Thank him that he is jealous for our attention and affection.
- Ask God to search your heart to reveal to you any particular sin that grieves his heart. Ask him to help you to deal with that sin.

# 33

# The Outpouring of the Spirit

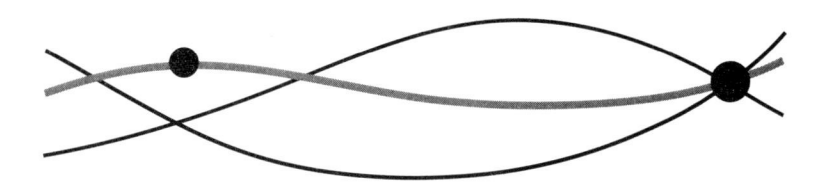

*Read Joel 2:28–32*

The result of repentance in the nation of Israel would be peace and prosperity in the land. This was only the beginning of what God had in store for his people. As God's people humbled themselves and repented of their sin, the Holy Spirit himself would be poured on them. What a day that would be. The words "and afterward" in verse 28 may indicate a leap in time to a distant future. Notice what Joel told his people would happen on that day.

The Holy Spirit would be poured on all people (verse 28). He would not come to Jews alone. This would not have been easy for the people of Joel's day to understand. They felt that salvation was for the Jew only, while the Gentile was unworthy of God's Spirit. The day was coming, however, when the Gentile would have an equal standing with the Jew.

When the Holy Spirit was poured out on the day of Pentecost, Peter told those gathered that what they were seeing a fulfillment of these words of Joel (Acts 2:16–21). Throughout the book of Acts, we see the Spirit of God coming to Gentile believers, much to the surprise of the Jews. We are seeing in our day the fulfillment of this prophecy as the Spirit of God reaches across racial and cultural barriers, bringing salvation and spiritual life to people of every nation and language.

Notice that God's Spirit would be poured out on all people regardless of social standing. In Old Testament times prophecy was a special gift given to a select group. When God wanted to speak to his people, he did so through his prophets. When the Spirit of God came this time, however, it would not be to a special group. This time he would fall on common people. Their sons and daughters would be touched by the Spirit of God and speak the word of God like the prophets. Their old men would have dreams from the Lord, as the Spirit of the Lord ministered to them. Even the lowest servants of their households would experience the outpouring of the Spirit of God on their lives. God's Spirit would not be limited to a select group but would come to the educated and the uneducated without distinction. Both the priest and the household servant would be empowered by the same Spirit.

God would show great wonders in the sky and on the earth (verses 30–31). These wonders would culminate in blood, fire, and smoke, suggesting warfare. As Joel prophesied that believers would be blessed, unbelievers would be judged. A day was coming when the sun would be turned to darkness and the moon to blood. This was a day to be feared. The light of the sun would be snuffed out by the breath of God. The moon's light would be no more. The inhabitants of the earth would be left in darkness. Terror and panic would fill the hearts of men and women as they came under the heavy hand of God's judgment. In other Scriptures, these are signs of divine presence and divine judgment (Exodus 19:16–18; Matthew 24:29–30; Revelation 6:12–17).

What are we to make of all this? Israel saw a partial fulfillment of this prophecy when she was invaded by the Assyrians and Babylonians and sent into exile. The ultimate fulfillment, however, is yet to come. Notice that this prophecy of judgment was to take place after the outpouring of the Holy Spirit. If the prophecy relating to the outpouring of the Spirit took place, as Peter said, in the day of Pentecost, it follows that we can expect that the remainder of this prophecy will see its fulfillment in the future when the unbelieving world will be judged by God.

Presently the Spirit of God is being poured out on every nation. People from every tribe and language are coming to know the Lord Jesus and receiving the Holy Spirit. Why was the Holy Spirit given to us? Acts 1:8 gives us the answer: "But you will receive power when the Holy Spirit comes on you; and you will be my witnesses in Jerusalem, and in all Judea and Samaria, and to the ends of the earth."

The Holy Spirit was given so that we can be witnesses for the Lord Jesus. The Holy Spirit comes to empower us to be witnesses to Christ and his work. We are living in exciting times. Since the day of Pentecost, the Holy Spirit of God has been calling and equipping saints and moving them out to the far corners of the earth with the message of the gospel. Never before has the world seen such a great movement of the Holy Spirit. Each day, all over the world, thousands of men, women, boys, and girls are coming to know Jesus. The Spirit of God is being poured out on all people.

We have seen that following the outpouring of God's Spirit there will be a day of judgment and accounting—a "dreadful day of the LORD" (verse 31). God now extends his gracious hand to each of us. Now is the day of salvation. Now, by his Spirit, he offers us peace with God and forgiveness of sin. The day is coming, however, when the whole world will be judged. Joel's prophecy is already partially fulfilled, and the remainder of his prophecy will also come to pass. We may even see this day of judgment in our lifetime.

The day of God's judgment will be a horrible day. It is described here as a day of blood, fire, and smoke. Maybe as you read this you are wondering how you can be sure that you will be safe on that day. Joel told his readers that there is a means of escape: "Everyone who calls on the name of the LORD would be saved."

What does it mean to call on the Lord? Picture a man hanging over the edge of a cliff, ready at any moment to fall to his death. He has come to the end of his human strength in his attempts to save himself. His hands are losing their grip, and he is ready at any moment to fall to his death. He now knows that it is impossible to save himself from his inevitable end. In despair he cries out for help, knowing that if ever he is going to be saved from this terrible disaster, it will only be at the hand of God. He calls out knowing that God alone is his hope.

Joel tells us that everyone who calls on the name of the Lord will be saved. Have you come to the end of your human resources? Do you realize that there is no hope of ever escaping the judgment of God by your own strength and good works? Do you feel your hands losing their grip? Are you aware of your inevitable end? It is to you that Joel is still speaking. There are many who call out to God who are not ready to abandon themselves completely to him. They still feel that they can save themselves. God may very well leave them to try. When they see this is impossible, they will then, in all sincerity, call out to him.

While in the first half of verse 32 Joel told his listeners that they needed to call out to the Lord to be saved, in the second half of the verse, he told them that deliverance would be for those whom the Lord called. Who does the calling here? Are we to call on the name of the Lord, or is he to call us? This verse tells us that both of these statements are true. As sinners we dare not approach a holy God without an invitation. In the days of the Persian Empire, only the person who was invited had the right to enter into the king's presence (see Esther 4:11). While the king had to first invite an individual into his presence, that individual had to accept the invitation.

When I called on the Lord for my salvation, I had the distinct impression that he was first calling me. I knew that he had placed his hand on my life and was melting away my resistance.

I called on him because he was first calling me. Our salvation is a combination of God's calling out to us individually and personally and our acceptance of that invitation by calling back or responding to him (see John 6:65; 1 John 4:19).

Have you ever heard that call from God? Has his Spirit been speaking to your heart? Has the King invited you into his presence? To reject his offer is to perish in sin. To accept it is to know forgiveness and freedom from eternal judgment. The remainder of Joel's prophecy will not delay in coming. Our only hope is to call on the name of the Lord. There is deliverance and freedom for all who hear his call and accept his invitation.

*For Consideration:*

- What change has the Holy Spirit made in your life? What evidence is there in your life of the presence of the Holy Spirit?

- How are you being a witness for the Lord Jesus today?

- What do we learn here about the judgment of God? Why do you suppose there is a diminishing emphasis in preaching today on the judgment to come?

- Why has God given us his Holy Spirit?

*For Prayer:*

- Take a moment to ask the Lord how you can reach out in the power of the Holy Spirit to someone who does not know him.

- Thank the Lord that he has given his Holy Spirit to empower and comfort us.

- Thank the Lord that he is a God of justice and holiness. Thank him that he will punish sin.

# 34

# The Valley of Jehoshaphat

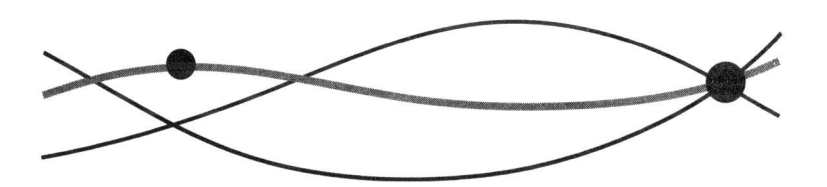

*Read Joel 3:1–16*

There is something about being in a family that unites the people involved. Brothers and sisters who cannot get along in normal times will stand up in defense of each other when attacked by an outsider. Joel prophesied that the day was coming when the great God of this universe would seek revenge on those who had insulted and harmed his children. God's people often rebelled against him, but they were still his family, and he would take their defense.

God called the nations to the Valley of Jehoshaphat (verse 2). The name Jehoshaphat means "the Lord judges." It is best to see this valley as a place of judgment and not a particular valley in Israel. In the Valley of Jehoshaphat (valley of judgment) the Lord God would bring his sentence against the nations who had oppressed his people.

God's people have, over the course of history, been oppressed by other nations. In biblical times the nations of Egypt, Assyria, Babylon, Persia, Greece, and Rome all played roles in persecuting and scattering God's people. In more recent history, many other nations have also oppressed God's chosen ones. By extension, the church too has suffered and will suffer at the hands of the nations. In the history of the church, God's people have lost homes and families for his cause. While at present we may not see justice in all this, God has not turned a blind eye to the hurts of his people. Joel prophesied that the day was coming when God would call the nations to account for their actions.

Notice how these foreign nations had treated the people of God. Verse 3 tells us that they cast lots for them. When the disciples were looking for a replacement for Judas, they chose two eligible men and cast lots to select one of them. In so doing, they were acting according to God's will (Acts 1:24–26). This is not the case here in Joel. These nations cast lots for God's people as the soldiers cast lots for the cloak of Jesus (Mark 15:24). They reduced the destiny of God's children to a game. Where was this Jew going to go? In whose house would he serve as slave? What about that beautiful young Jewish girl? Who was going to get her? To decide, they played a game. The winner got his pick. How humiliating this was for the people of God. As God watched this whole procedure, his anger boiled within him. A day of accounting was coming. These nations would answer for what they had done to the children of the King.

This dehumanization can also be seen in how they treated the young Jewish children. To satisfy their sexual appetites, these foreigners traded boys for prostitutes (verse 3). These men cared nothing about the future of these young boys. They were willing to subject them to a lifetime of abuse for a moment of pleasure. God was justly angered by this treatment of his people.

While the young Jewish boys were being traded for prostitutes, the young Jewish girls were being traded for wine in verse 3. What would happen to these young girls? Either they would be reduced to slavery or sexually abused. Once again, the nations cared nothing about these young girls. They traded a young Jewish girl for a bottle of wine. To satisfy their lust for alcohol, they were willing to subject a young girl to a lifetime of slavery or sexual abuse. God would take vengeance on these crimes against his people.

In verse 4 God passes his sentence on the people of Tyre, Sidon, and the region of Philistia. "Now what have you against me?" God asked. "Are you repaying me for something I have done?" God so identified with his people that to touch them was to touch him. These nations could be sure of one thing—their judgment would come swiftly. The nations were accused of stealing God's wealth when they took what God had given to his people. They stripped God's temple of its gold and silver and took it to adorn their own temples (verse 5). They were a greedy people. They adorned themselves at the expense of others. For this, God would judge them.

In verse 6 we read that these nations did not hesitate to sell the Jews to the Greeks. These Greeks took them far away from the land God had given them as an inheritance. God saw what was taking place. God would return on their heads what they had done to his people (verse 7). God's people would return to their land. God would endow them with strength, and they would become his instruments in rendering justice to the nations. They would do to the nations what the nations had done to them. This is the spiritual principle of reaping what is sown (Galatians 6:7).

A call went forth in verse 9. It was a call to arms. The warriors were aroused from their sleep. The fighting men of the nations were to assemble for immediate attack. The people of the land were to gather anything that could be made into a weapon of war. Plowshares and pruning hooks were to be shaped into spears and swords (verse 10). Even the weaklings and cowards were to stand up and fight for their lives.

The nations were to gather in the Valley of Jehoshaphat (verses 11–12). There God would swing the sickle of his righteous anger. The time of harvest would come. Like grapes placed in the wine press, the Lord would trample his enemies until their blood, like juice, overflowed the vats and spilled over the side.

Joel foresaw the day of judgment. Multitudes would gather before the Lord in the valley of decision where the Lord would decide their fate (verse 14). The sun and the stars would cease to shine (verse 15). The earth would be cast into the blackness of divine wrath. The land would tremble as the Lord moved out in judgment on the nations. This would be a terrible day of wrath. The only ones who would be safe on that day were the people of God (verse 16). God would be a refuge and stronghold for them.

What do these verses teach us today? They teach us two important lessons. The first of these lessons relates to how much the Lord loves his people. The reason for this terrible judgment was because of how the nations treated God's children. In the prophecy of Zechariah 2:8, God told his people that anyone who touched them was touching the "apple of his eye." Similarly, Jesus told his readers in Matthew 25:40 that what we do to the least of his children we do to him: "The King will reply, 'I tell you the truth, whatever you did for one of the least of these brothers of mine, you did for me.'"

This is a terrifying thought. How we need to understand that God takes it very personally when we mistreat one of his children. He will hold us accountable for how we treat his loved ones. This section of Joel shows us how angry God becomes when his people are hurt.

This passage teaches us also that there is a day of judgment coming. Verse 16 tells us that the Lord will be a refuge and a stronghold for his people on that day of wrath. Only his children will escape unharmed. Are you sure today that you are a child of God? You need to be sure. Only his children will pass through this judgment. We do not know when this day will come on us. When it comes it will be too late. Now is the time to become a child of God. This is not something you can do for yourself. You have no more power to become a child of God than you had to become a child of your earthly parents.

How, then, can you become a child of God? You must recognize that you will never get to heaven as you are. In your natural state, you are a child of this world, and this world is at enmity with God. You need to be born again spiritually as a new person. This new spiritual life is the life of the Spirit of God who takes up residence in you when you ask God to save you. This life is a gift of God offered freely to all who truly call on him. What a difference it makes when this gift of new life is given. As his children, we are forgiven, and our future is secure.

*For Consideration:*

- What does this section teach us about the importance of maintaining a good relationship with fellow believers?

- What do we learn here about how God thinks about us as his children?

- What encouragement do you find in the fact that God will judge sin and evil? Where would we be today if God did not judge sin? Could we trust such a God?

*For Prayer:*

- If you have never experienced new life in Christ, call on him now asking him to make you his child.

- If you have been guilty of offending a child of God, ask for forgiveness.

- Is there someone you have trouble loving? Ask God for strength to love his children as he loves them.

# 35

# A Bright Future for God's People

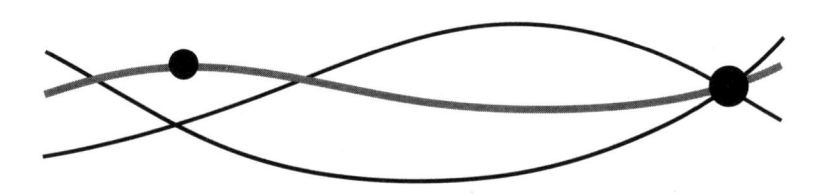

*Read Joel 3:17–21*

Joel began his prophecy by reminding God's people of a great swarm of locusts coming to devour their land. These locusts would devastate everything in their path. God would lead this great force into judgment against his people (1:1–2:11). The result would be that his people would repent of their sin and turn to him. God would restore them and forgive their sin (2:12–27). When he had restored his people, God would then draw near to them and pour out his Spirit on them (2:28–32). During the days following the outpouring of his Spirit, God would enter into judgment against the nations who had oppressed his chosen ones (3:1–16). He would grant his people justice. When all these things took place, the people of God would know that God was truly in their midst (verse 17).

There were, no doubt, many times when the people of God wondered if God was really there. As the locusts invaded the land, they wondered if God really loved them. When their children were being sold as slaves and carried away from the land the Lord had promised them, no doubt, they wondered whether the Lord had abandoned them. In time, however, they would see that the Lord is always faithful to his promises.

Maybe you are in a similar situation today. Maybe you just can't believe that the Lord really loves you. "If he loved me," you say, "why does he allow me to suffer as I do?" This is a legitimate question. It is a question we cannot presently answer. In time, however, as we remain faithful, we will see that the Lord does care. We will see how our pain fits into his great overall plan. When the time is right you too will know that God does indeed "dwell in Zion" (verse 17). He is seated on his throne. He works out all things for our good.

Joel prophesied that the day was coming when Jerusalem would be holy. What does it mean to be holy? Holiness refers to being consecrated to God and his will for our lives. In that day foreigners would no longer invade God's people. The day was coming when God's people would be free from anything or anyone who would seek to harm them or take them away from their God. While this passage may have a literal earthly fulfillment for the Jewish people in a millennial kingdom, it also has a deep spiritual significance for all of us who are God's people. In Revelation 21:1–4 the apostle John speaks of a New Jerusalem coming down from heaven.

> Then I saw a new heaven and a new earth, for the first heaven and the first earth had passed away, and there was no longer any sea. I saw the Holy City, the new Jerusalem, coming down out of heaven from God, prepared as a bride beautifully dressed for her husband. And I heard a loud voice from the throne saying, "Now the dwelling of God is with men, and he will live with them. They will be his people, and God himself will be with them and be their God. He will wipe every tear from their eyes. There will be no more death or mourning or crying or pain, for the old order of things has passed away."

John reminds us in the above passage that the presence of the Lord would dwell in this New Jerusalem. There would be no more tears. No foreigner to the grace of God would ever be allowed to enter the city. According to Revelation 21:25–27, only those who are holy, that is, consecrated to God, will dwell there. "On no day will its gates ever be shut, for there will be no night there. The glory and honor of the nations will be brought into it. Nothing impure will ever enter it, nor will anyone who does what is shameful or deceitful, but only those whose names are written in the Lamb's book of life."

What a wonderful promise God gives to his people. All believers will share in the blessings promised to Israel. We too will dwell in this New Jerusalem in the presence of God where we will live in perfect peace and contentment.

Joel went on to describe holy Jerusalem in verse 18. The mountains of this city would drip with new wine. New wine comes from a fresh crop of grapes. This is a sign of real prosperity. Prior to this the locusts had stripped the land bare. Their new wine was dried up (1:10). The day was coming when God's people would live in prosperity and abundance. The earth would be released from its curse and produce her crops in abundance.

Joel 1:18 tells us that, in the day of God's wrath, the cattle moaned because they had no pasture. When the cattle have no pasture, they do not produce milk. The day was coming, however, when the hills would again spring forth with green grass. The cattle would graze in these green pastures. They would, in turn, produce an abundance of milk. This again is a sign of the rich blessing of God on the land.

Joel 1:20 tells us that the streams of the land had dried up. There was no water for the people to drink. All around them was a dry, barren wasteland. The day was coming when all this would change. The rains of God's blessing would again be poured down on the earth, quenching the thirst of the dried wasteland and overflowing into the streams and rivers of the land. The desert would become a garden. The wasteland would flourish with abundant crops. God's people would quench their thirst and bathe in the abundance of fresh water.

In those days a fountain would flow out of the house of the Lord and water the valley of acacias (Valley of Shittim, KJV). The word *shittim* is the Hebrew word for "acacias." This water comes from the house of the Lord. There is no question as to the source of this blessing. God himself sent this fountain to water the great acacia trees. It may be of significance that acacia wood was used in the construction of the tabernacle (Exodus 25).

What we see here is a picture of prosperity and blessing flowing from the throne of God. God's people are free from their enemies and live in a land flowing with new wine and milk. Verse 20 tells us that their land would be inhabited forever. No one would be able to take away their inheritance. Their sins would be forgiven, and they would live forever in peace with God (verse 21). As for the nations that had oppressed God's people, theirs was a different future. For example, Egypt would be desolate, and Edom would become a desert wasteland (verse 19).

As we have walked our way through this prophecy of Joel, we have moved from a barren wasteland devoured by locusts in chapter 1 to a land flowing with new wine and milk in chapter 3. The transition from barrenness to blessing comes in chapter 2 where Israel recognized her sin and returned to the Lord for forgiveness. All that separated her from the outpouring of God's abundance was her need of forgiveness. That forgiveness was given freely to her when she repented.

Maybe you are in the same situation today. Has your experience been one of desolation and spiritual barrenness? There is hope for you in the book of Joel. God desires to pour his Spirit on you. His Spirit will quench all the thirsty places in your heart and fill you to overflowing with peace and spiritual prosperity. Before the pouring out of the Spirit, however, there is a call to repentance. Repentance is all that separates you from the great blessing of God in your life. Joel places before us an option.

What will it be? Will it be locusts, or will it be new wine?

*For Consideration:*

- What blessings did Joel promise to those who repent of their sin? Are you experiencing these blessings today?

- Describe some changes that have come about in your life since you came to Christ.

- What role does repentance have in the restoration of blessings to God's people?

- What picture did Joel give us of heaven here in this final section of his prophecy?

*For Prayer:*

- Take a moment to thank the Lord for the bright future that awaits all those who put their trust in him.

- Ask God to reveal any sin in you that separates you from his richest blessing.

- Ask God to help you to live daily with a repentant heart.